Essential Histories

The Rise of Imperial Rome
AD 14–193

Essential Histories

The Rise of Imperial Rome
AD 14–193

Duncan B Campbell

First published in Great Britain in 2013 by Osprey Publishing,
Midland House, West Way, Botley, Oxford, OX2 0PH, UK
43-01 21st Street, Suite 220B, Long Island City, NY 11101 USA
E-mail: info@ospreypublishing.com

Osprey Publishing is part of the Osprey Group

A CIP catalogue record for this book is available from the British
Library

Print ISBN: 978 1 78096 280 1
PDF ebook ISBN: 978 1 78096 281 8
ePub ebook ISBN: 978 1 78096 282 5

Page layouts by Myriam Bell Design, UK
Index by Angela Hall
Typeset in ITC Stone Serif and Gill Sans
Maps by Peter Bull Art Studio
Originated by PDQ Media, Bungay, UK
Printed in China through Asia Pacific Offset Limited

13 14 15 16 17   10 9 8 7 6 5 4 3 2 1

Dedication

To all my friends at Indigo Childcare, who think I'm an architect.

Editor's note

All translations into English are the author's. All illustrations not
otherwise credited are via iStock.

Abbreviations

AE	*L'Année épigraphique* (Paris, 1889–)
CIL	T. Mommsen et al., *Corpus Inscriptionum Latinarum* (Berlin, 1863–)
ILS	H. Dessau, *Inscriptiones Latinae Selectae* (Berlin, 1892–1916)
RMD 5	P. Holder, *Roman Military Diplomas* V (London, 2006)

Osprey Publishing is supporting the Woodland Trust, the UK's
leading woodland conservation charity, by funding the dedication
of trees.

www.ospreypublishing.com

Contents

Introduction

During the reign of Hadrian, the great Roman historian Publius Cornelius Tacitus wrote what would be his final work, entitled the *Annals*: it is a chronicle of Roman history from the death of Augustus to the death of Nero. In it he lamented that, while the historians of the Roman Republic had written about 'great wars, the storming of cities, and the capture of vanquished kings', his own themes were 'restricted and inglorious: peace, undisturbed or scarcely challenged, depressing events in the city, and an emperor uninterested in extending the empire' (*Annals* 4.32, referring to the emperor Tiberius).

Tacitus had grown up under the Flavian emperors. He served out a moderately successful senatorial career, perhaps beginning with a tribunate in one of the legions that spearheaded the invasion of Caledonia under his father-in-law, Gnaeus Julius Agricola. Having risen to the consulship under the emperor Nerva, he went on to hold the prestigious proconsulship of Asia towards the end of Trajan's reign. He had thus lived through a time of great wars, but – unfortunately for us – never took the opportunity to write of Trajan's storming of cities (both in Dacia and in Parthia) and the capture of the vanquished Dacian king Decebalus.

A generation or so before Tacitus, Pliny the encyclopaedist had celebrated 'the boundless majesty of the Roman peace' (*Natural History* 27.3), which enabled men and goods to criss-cross the entire world in safety. However, when Tacitus claims that this peace was 'undisturbed or scarcely challenged', he exaggerates. A chronological survey of the military exploits of successive emperors demonstrates that, for all the talk of *pax Romana* ('the Roman peace'), conflict rumbled constantly around the periphery of the empire, occasionally flaring into full-scale war. Tacitus was well aware of this. Even in his own lifetime, the steady roll call of senators honoured with *ornamenta triumphalia* ('triumphal ornaments'), the inexorable increase in each emperor's imperatorial acclamations (each one a sign that success had been won in warfare somewhere in the empire), and the fact that the great double doors of the Temple of Janus, required by tradition to be closed in times of peace, stood ajar for years on end – all of these elements demonstrated that the rise of the Roman empire was not accomplished by peaceful means.

The first two centuries of the Roman empire may have ushered in a period of peace for the citizens of Rome, but the ruling elite – the senators and equestrians who did the emperor's bidding – still required their opportunity to win glory, even if victories were now won under the auspices of the emperor. More important than *pax Romana*, to these men, was *Victoria Augusta* ('the emperor's victory'). Year by year and decade by decade, successful emperors managed the affairs on the frontiers in a way that ensured the winning of glory for these men, while emperors who were 'uninterested' failed to see the dangers of ignoring these potential rivals. Our chronological survey reveals the depressing cycle of success and failure in the rise of imperial Rome.

Trajan's Column was completed in AD 113. The relief sculpture wrapped around the 100ft exterior tells the story of Trajan's two Dacian Wars. Inside, a staircase spirals up to a viewing platform at the top. On the emperor's death in AD 117, his ashes (and subsequently those of his widow, Plotina) were deposited inside the base.

Chronology

27 BC–AD 14	Reign of Augustus
26–25 BC	Campaign of Aelius Gallus in Arabia Felix; campaign of Publius Carisius in north-western Spain
25 BC	Campaign of Aulus Terentius Varro Murena in the Alps; establishment of Galatia as a province following death of its king
24 BC	Campaign of Lucius Aelius Lamia in north-western Spain
24–22 BC	Campaign of Gaius Petronius in Ethiopia
19 BC	Campaign of Lucius Cornelius Balbus in north Africa (the last private citizen to be granted a 'triumph'); Marcus Agrippa completes pacification of Spain
17–16 BC	Campaigns of Publius Silius Nerva in the Alps
16 BC	Loss of legion in Gaul under Marcus Lollius
15 BC	Campaigns of Tiberius and Drusus in the Alps and Raetia; probable establishment of Noricum as a province
14 BC	Establishment of Alpes Maritimae as a province
13 BC	Campaign of Marcus Agrippa in Illyricum
12–9 BC	Campaign of Tiberius in Balkans
12–5 BC	Campaigns beyond the Rhine
11–9 BC	Revolt in Thrace suppressed by Lucius Calpurnius Piso
AD 4–5	Campaigns beyond the Rhine briefly resumed
AD 6	Establishment of Judaea as a province; warfare in north Africa; creation of the *aerarium militare* to pay military pensions
AD 6–9	Revolt in Pannonia and Illyricum suppressed by Tiberius
AD 9	Loss of three legions in Teutoberg Forest in Germany under Publius Quinctilius Varus
AD 14	Establishment of the military zones on the upper and lower Rhine; probable establishment of Pannonia as a province; army revolts in Illyricum and along Rhine on news of Augustus' death
AD 14–37	Reign of Tiberius
AD 15–16	Campaign of Germanicus across the Rhine
AD 16	Battle of Idistaviso; won by Germanicus
AD 17	Establishment of Cappadocia as a province, after death of its king
AD 17–24	Revolt of Tacfarinas in north Africa finally suppressed by Publius Cornelius Dolabella
AD 21	Revolt of Florus and Sacrovir in Gaul suppressed by Gaius Silius Largus

AD 24	Battle of Auzea, won by Publius Cornelius Dolabella
AD 25	Probable establishment of Raetia as a province
AD 28	Revolt of the Frisii; defeat of Lucius Apronius
AD 37–41	Reign of Gaius (Caligula)
AD 39	Third Augusta Legion removed from the command of the proconsul of Africa
AD 39–40	Caligula's manoeuvres on the Rhine and North Sea coast
AD 40	Establishment of Mauretania as a province, after death of its king
AD 41–54	Reign of Claudius
AD 41	Campaign of Servius Sulpicius Galba and Publius Gabinius Secundus across the Rhine
AD 42	Reorganization of Mauretania as two provinces; revolt of Lucius Arruntius Scribonianus in Dalmatia
AD 43	Invasion of Britain under Aulus Plautius; establishment of Lycia–Pamphilia as a province
AD 44	Establishment of Moesia as a province; establishment of Britannia as a province (although conquest continues)
AD 46	Establishment of Thracia as a province, after death of its king
AD 54–68	Reign of Nero
AD 58–63	Parthian crisis twice defused by Gnaeus Domitius Corbulo
AD 60	Revolt of Boudica in Britannia suppressed by Gaius Suetonius Paullinus
AD 62	Surrender of a Roman army under Lucius Caesennius Paetus to the Parthians at Rhandeia
AD 63	Establishment of Alpes Cottiae as a province following the death of its king
AD 66–74	First Jewish War
AD 68	Revolt of Gaius Julius Vindex in Gaul, suppressed by Lucius Verginius Rufus
AD 69	Year of the Four Emperors; first and second battles of Cremona
AD 69–79	Reign of Vespasian
AD 70	Batavian Revolt suppressed by Quintus Petillius Cerialis; siege of Jerusalem by Titus
AD 72	Province of Cappadocia expanded to include the kingdom of Commagene following the deposition of its king
AD 74	Siege of Masada by Lucius Flavius Silva
AD 79–81	Reign of Titus
AD 81–96	Reign of Domitian
AD 83	Battle of Mons Graupius, won by Gnaeus Julius Agricola
AD 83–85	Chattan War
AD 85–89	Domitian's Dacian War
AD 86	Province of Moesia split into Moesia Superior and Moesia Inferior

AD **88**   First battle of Tapae, won by
              Lucius Tettius Julianus

AD **89**   Revolt of Lucius Antonius
              Saturninus on the upper Rhine

AD **90**   Formal creation of the provinces of
              Germania Superior and Germania
              Inferior out of the military zones
              on the Rhine (approximate date)

AD **96–98**   Reign of Nerva

AD **98–117** Reign of Trajan

AD **101–02** Trajan's First Dacian War

AD **101**   Second battle of Tapae

AD **105–06** Second Dacian War; establishment
              of Dacia as a province

AD **106**   Province of Pannonia divided
              into Pannonia Superior and
              Pannonia Inferior; establishment
              of Arabia as a province

AD **114–15** Trajan's Parthian War

AD **117–38** Reign of Hadrian

AD **117–18** Province of Dacia split into Dacia
              Superior, Dacia Inferior and (now
              or slightly later) Dacia Porolissensis

AD **122**   Hadrian's Wall begun
              (approximate date)

AD **132–35** Second Jewish War; province of
              Judaea renamed Syria Palaestina

AD **138–61** Reign of Antoninus Pius

AD **139**   Expansion of Britannia into
              lowland Scotland

AD **140**   Antonine Wall begun

AD **145–52** Moorish War

AD **156–58** Antonius Pius' Dacian War

AD **161–69** Joint reign of Marcus Aurelius
              and Lucius Verus

AD **161**   Battle of Elegeia, lost by
              Marcus Sedatius Severianus

AD **162–66** Lucius Verus' Parthian War

AD **167**   Dacian provinces united into a
              single province of Three Dacias

AD **167–75** Marcomannic Wars

AD **169–80** Sole reign of Marcus Aurelius

AD **170**   Invasion of Italy by Marcomanni
              and Quadi

AD **175**   Revolt of Avidius Cassius in
              Syria suppressed by Publius
              Martius Verus

AD **178–80** Marcomannic Wars resumed

AD **180–92** Reign of Commodus

AD **193**   Reign of Pertinax

AD **193–211** Reign of Septimius Severus

AD **194**   Province of Syria split into
              Syria Phoenice and Syria Coele

AD **195**   Establishment of Osrhoene as
              a province

AD **197**   Province of Britannia split into
              Britannia Superior and Britannia
              Inferior; establishment of
              Mesopotamia as a province

AD **198**   Formal creation of the province
              of Numidia

The Roman empire in AD 14

The first emperor

When Augustus (r. 27 BC–AD 14) came to the throne as the first emperor of Rome, he began to bring order to the chaos that 20 years of civil war had wrought. The old Republican system of rule by the senate, with its two annually elected consuls, still functioned, but had proved vulnerable to manipulation by powerful individuals. During the mid-1st century BC, Julius Caesar in particular had subverted the senate by carefully amassing personal power, at first through the agency of a triumvirate ('rule by three men', which he came to dominate), and then by becoming *dictator perpetuo* ('dictator for life') in 44 BC. Consequently, the Roman populace had become used to autocratic rule.

Caesar's example was followed by his adopted son and heir, Augustus, who – initially going by the name Caesar, in the aftermath of the dictator's assassination in 44 BC – swore 'to attain his father's honours' (Cicero, *Letters to Atticus* 16.15.3). Although no less ambitious, the new Caesar was perhaps more savvy. He moved from being a member of a triumvirate – whose supreme authority was carefully disguised in its remit 'to restore the Republic' – to being the saviour of Italy from the clutches of an orientalized Mark Antony (whom he defeated at the naval battle of Actium in 31 BC). But he always downplayed the extent of his power. 'After I extinguished the fires of civil war', he later wrote, 'having taken control of affairs in accordance with the wishes of my fellow citizens, I transferred the Republic from my own power into the arbitration of the senate and people of Rome' (*The Achievements of the Divine Augustus* 34.1).

As an 'ordinary citizen' – he referred to himself only as *princeps* ('the first citizen'),

from which this period of history has become known as the Principate – the new Caesar made sure to remain in the public eye, first by monopolizing the annual consulship (but only until 23 BC), and secondly by staging three ostentatious triumphal processions, reminding everyone of his victories in Illyricum in 34–33 BC and at Actium in 31 BC, and of his subsequent capture of Egypt from Cleopatra, last of the Ptolemies. Then, having been voted the name Augustus ('sacred one') in 27 BC, he began (cunningly but tactfully)

The famous statue of Augustus, discovered at Livia's villa at Prima Porta near Rome. The sculpted cuirass depicts the handing over of a Roman battle-standard, thought to represent those lost to the Parthians by Crassus in 53 BC, which were returned to Augustus in 20 BC. (UIG via Getty Images)

to accumulate a range of traditional Republican offices, which would (legally but unobtrusively) guarantee the continuation of his authority at Rome.

Like the magistrates of old, he was granted a *provincia* ('sphere of authority', usually implying the temporary governorship of a geographical territory), except that Augustus' province extended across Spain and Gaul in the west, and Syria and Egypt in the east, encompassing all the armies that were located there, and, although technically temporary, gradually became permanent. He arranged this 'on the pretext that the senate might enjoy the best parts of the empire without anxiety, while he himself took on the hardships and hazards', as the historian Cassius Dio explained, 'but the real object of this arrangement was that the senators should be unarmed and unequipped for battle, while he alone possessed arms and maintained soldiers' (*Roman History* 53.12.3). This ulterior motive is compelling, for, by this stage, only one Roman legion lay outside the emperor's domain and took its orders from the annually elected proconsul of Africa.

Of course, the government of Rome was still the preserve of the senatorial class, the landed aristocracy of which Augustus and his successors were all members. But the new emperor began to involve their equestrian counterparts – those families who either could not afford to join the senatorial order (there was a property qualification of one million sesterces, whereas an equestrian required only a net worth of 400,000 sesterces, at a time when the common man might earn 500 sesterces a year) or chose not to. This move was ostensibly to widen the pool of available army officers, but fortuitously served as a surreptitious foil to the senatorial monopoly on power. The important governorship of Egypt, with its agrarian wealth (on one estimate, as much as one-third of Rome's grain came from Egypt), was entrusted to an equestrian *praefectus* ('prefect'), rather than a senatorial proconsul or a *legatus* ('legate'), even though special provision

had to be made to bring his powers into line with his senatorial counterparts.

In 23 BC, although Augustus now stepped down from the consulship, he took the *tribunicia potestas* ('power of a tribune'), referring to the tribune of the plebs, an annually renewed office that had symbolic overtones of 'the people's champion'; more importantly, besides conferring *sacrosanctitas* ('immunity from prosecution'), it granted Augustus the practical privilege of vetoing any proposals in the senate. Each of his successors made sure that they acquired this power and, more importantly, that they renewed it every year.

All of the titles, honours and functions taken by Augustus formed the basis of the legal authority that successive Roman emperors would wield. Their power, though absolute, was firmly based in Republican tradition. The long reign of Augustus, which lasted over 40 years, gave the new regime time to become embedded in the Roman consciousness. Furthermore, Augustus' decision to implement a dynastic succession by adopting his stepson Tiberius as his chosen heir, and bestowing the *tribunicia potestas* upon him, influenced the future direction of the Roman Principate. It would be many years before the *arcanus imperii* ('secret of empire') was divulged: namely, as Tacitus put it, that 'an emperor could be made elsewhere than at Rome' (*Histories* 1.4).

A military regime

Augustus himself emphasized that 'I excelled everyone in *auctoritas* ['influence'], although I possessed no more official power than others who were my colleagues' (*The Achievements of the Divine Augustus* 34.3). Indeed, his senatorial colleagues continued to play their traditional role in government, though Augustus, by force of his *auctoritas*, was able to influence their decisions. Senators continued to occupy the main military and civil offices, such as legionary commands and provincial governorships, but most of these now operated within the emperor's *provincia*, and thus fell under his overall control. To be sure, the emperor could (and often did) summon a *consilium* ('council') of advisors, but was under no obligation to do so.

Patronage had always played a major part in Roman society. Every senator had his clients, who paid their respects in return for favours and benefits. Under the Principate, the emperor became a super-patron with the power to make or break men's careers. A young man's entry to the senatorial career itself was in the gift of the emperor. His provincial governors were styled 'friends' (*amici*), though the friendship was sometimes false: the 1st-century philosopher Epictetus observed that 'No one loves Caesar himself, unless he is particularly worthy, but we love wealth and tribunates, praetorships, consulships' (*Discourses* 4.1.60), referring to the various favours that the emperor might bestow. There was a kind of trickle-down effect, whereby those favoured by the emperor could, in turn, favour others. Thus, for example, the well-connected senator might petition the emperor for lucrative posts on behalf of friends and relatives, and the governor of a military province appears to have had a free hand in appointing his officers (though probably only below the rank of legionary commander).

Augustus had bought the favour of the populace at Rome with the generous provision of 'bread and games' (as this form of bribery was later summed up by the poet Juvenal) and grandiose building schemes: not only temples and porticoes, but public baths and an improved water and sewerage system. Meanwhile, the favour of the armies was bought with regular pay and generous pensions; both were necessary to compensate the soldiers for long service on far-flung frontiers. In 30 BC after Actium, and again in 14 BC, large numbers of veterans had earned their discharge and expected their loyalty to be rewarded. Consequently, time-served soldiers were each granted a parcel of land on the colonies that Augustus founded up and down Italy. However, later programmes of discharge offered the men

a cash gratuity instead, perhaps amounting to ten years' pay; this enormous financial burden was paid out of Augustus' newly created *aerarium militare* ('military treasury').

It was surely to impress the armies that Augustus, early on, took as his first name the honorific title *imperator* ('conquering general'), the term by which a successful commander had traditionally been hailed by his army. (Indeed, this is the word from which 'emperor' comes.) At the same time, Augustus took over sole responsibility for issuing state coinage – which was, after all, principally used for paying the armies – and carefully manipulated its physical appearance to promote himself. Coins now bore an ageless likeness of his head – continuing Julius Caesar's break with Republican practice, which had never permitted the depiction of a living Roman – along with brief legends subtly emphasizing his authority (for example, CAESAR AVGVSTVS, stressing his link with Julius Caesar, or COMM CONS, claiming that he ruled *communi consensu*, 'by common consent').

Augustus continued the Republican tradition of the commander's bodyguard, surrounding himself and his family with a personal force of *Germani corporis custodes* ('Germanic bodyguard', mostly of Batavian origin) and stationing individual cohorts of *praetoriani* ('Praetorian Guard', alluding to the *praetorium* or military headquarters of the emperor) in and around Rome. He also instituted two key paramilitary organizations in Rome, the *urbaniciani* ('urban cohorts') and the *vigiles* ('night watchmen'), whose roles were, respectively, those of a police force and a fire brigade, broadly speaking. The Praetorian Guard was another institution that Augustus was perhaps wary of placing in senatorial hands, for the powerful *praefectus praetorio* (the Praetorian prefect), effectively the emperor's right-hand man, was always a senior equestrian. Often, two *praefecti* were appointed, so that the Guard might be divided (or so that each prefect could watch the other).

The legions – once upon a time mobilized only during times of trouble, their ranks

The Roman world in 27 BC

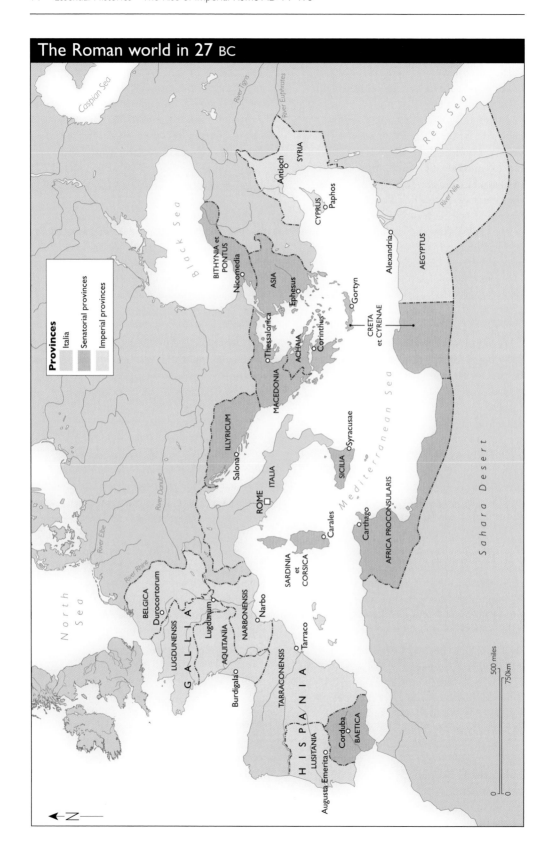

filled by peasant citizens, eager for adventure and booty, and just as eager to return to their Italian farms – had, in many cases, become long-service regiments, whose recruits, drawn from the more Romanized provinces, were loyal to their paymaster. Under Augustus, this ad hoc situation became regularized and incorporated into his vision of empire: a fixed number of permanently constituted legions were henceforth stationed in the frontier provinces. Similarly, the smaller units of 'auxiliaries' – raised among the more warlike peoples on the fringes of the Roman world

mostly to supplement the legions' deficiencies in cavalry and missile troops – were gradually standardized and brought within the same system. However, where the legions were entrusted largely to senatorial officers, it became usual to entrust the auxiliary units to equestrians, thus satisfying each order's desire for status and glory.

A firm foundation

When Augustus died in AD 14, the Roman empire inherited by Tiberius already spread far and wide across the Mediterranean world. Over the course of the previous two centuries, areas had been added piecemeal to the Italian core as the Romans meddled in the affairs of other nations. First, the Carthaginian possessions in Spain and north Africa were absorbed; then Greece and Macedonia, and

The *Gemma Augustea* cameo depicts Augustus (in the upper register) in the guise of Jupiter 'Best and Greatest', seated beside the goddess Roma, while Roman soldiers (in the lower register) erect a victory trophy amid their defeated enemies. Augustus' capricorn emblem appears above his head, while Tiberius' scorpio emblem appears on a shield (bottom left). (De Agostini/Getty Images)

Gallia Narbonensis; and, in the east, Syria and parts of Asia Minor.

Augustus himself brought order to Caesar's conquests in Gaul and, although he omitted to capitalize on Caesar's contacts with the Britons on the very edge of the known world, he pushed Roman arms across the Rhine into Germany; his general Lucius Domitius Ahenobarbus (grandfather of the future emperor Nero) had even led an army across the River Elbe, for which he received *ornamenta triumphalia* ('triumphal ornaments', the triumph itself being now restricted to the emperor and his family). By now, Germania Magna ('greater Germany' beyond the Rhine) was, in the words of the historian Velleius

Paterculus, 'almost reduced to the form of a tribute-paying province' (*Roman History* 2.97.4), but when the project was entrusted to Publius Quinctilius Varus, it met with disaster in the Teutoburg Forest in AD 9.

Elsewhere, long years of hard campaigning finally saw Tarraconensis and Illyricum (soon to be renamed Dalmatia) become fully-fledged provinces, and softened up the areas north of the Alps, which were destined to become the provinces of Noricum, Raetia and Pannonia. At the same time, the Roman administration in Macedonia occasionally became involved in affairs to the north, in the area that would later become Moesia.

The Rhine and Danube marked a clear boundary between the Roman empire and the peoples beyond, although successive emperors still exercised a claim over those peoples. Similarly, the Euphrates had become the *de facto* line of demarcation between Rome and the Parthian empire, which stretched eastwards across Iran. Nevertheless, Augustus artfully created the impression in the minds of his contemporaries that Rome ruled the entire world. During his reign, writers wrote in terms of *imperium sine fine* ('an empire without end'), and Augustus himself claimed to have subdued the world. 'Everywhere throughout the human race', wrote the historian Florus, 'there was either

peace or pact, stable and uninterrupted, and Caesar Augustus finally ventured to close the double doors of the Temple of Janus' (*Epitome of Roman History* 2.34), which traditionally stood open while the Romans were at war and had last been closed over two centuries before.

The ruling class in Italy certainly welcomed an end to the troubled years of civil war. 'When peace was established throughout the world and the republic was restored', runs the text of a contemporary funeral eulogy, 'times were quiet and happy for us' (*ILS* 8393) – but not, apparently, for Augustus, wearied towards the end of his long reign (in the words of Pliny the encyclopaedist) by 'the conjunction of so many misfortunes' (*Natural History* 7.149). Chief among them was, of course, the *clades Variana* ('disaster of Varus'), in which three legions were destroyed in the trackless wilderness beyond the Rhine; the distraught emperor, by now a septuagenarian, was said to 'dash his head, from time to time, against the door, crying out: "Quinctilius Varus, give me back my legions!"' (Suetonius, *Life of the Deified Augustus* 23.2).

It was surely in the context of this disaster that Augustus allegedly passed on the following advice to his successors: 'he advised them to be satisfied with the present conditions and not to wish to increase the empire further, for it would then be difficult to guard, and he thought that they would run the risk of losing what was already theirs' (Cassius Dio, *Roman History* 56.33.5). This 'advice to confine the empire within its boundaries' (the version preserved by Tacitus, *Annals* 1.11) jars with the Roman desire for glory and the belief in *imperium sine fine*, and its authenticity has been questioned by modern historians. In any case, each successive emperor can be seen to have formulated his own 'Grand Strategy'.

Roman cavalry skirmish on this bas-relief panel on the north face of the Mausoleum of the Julii at Glanum (near modern Saint-Rémy-de-Provence), dating from around 25 BC. The Roman four-horned saddle can clearly be seen on the riderless horse. (SiefkinDR/CC-BY-SA-3.0)

Rome and her enemies

The Roman army

The Roman army had always been built around the citizen legions of heavily armed and armoured infantry. During the civil war that eventually ushered in the Principate, the rival leaders had been building up their own armies, so that the total number of legions under arms had reached about 60. Each had its own number (though rival leaders had followed their own numbering sequences) and many had honorific names (the so-called *cognomina*, or 'surnames') that recalled past battle honours. One of the tasks that Augustus set himself was to create an effective standing army for his new Roman empire by disbanding more than half of these legions and pensioning off their personnel.

On account of its imperfect origins, the resulting legionary army – which numbered 25 legions at the death of Augustus – contained several duplicate numbers.

For example, there was a Fourth Macedonica Legion, stationed in Spain until Claudius' invasion of Britain brought it to the upper Rhine, where it replaced the Fourteenth Gemina at Mogontiacum (present-day Mainz); but there was also a Fourth Scythica Legion, stationed in the Balkans until it moved east during Nero's Armenian crisis. Augustus' army contained duplicate Fifth, Sixth, and Tenth legions, and he even retained three Third legions: the Third Augusta, which remained the garrison of north Africa for the entire period of the Principate; the Third Cyrenaica, which was stationed in Egypt until Trajan transferred it to his new province of Arabia; and the

The west corner of the legionary fortress of Isca (present-day Caerleon in Wales), where the foundations of four barrack blocks have been consolidated. Each was designed for a single *centuria*, with around eight men sharing a double cubicle, while their centurion occupied the more generous suite of rooms at the end. To the left of the corner tower, a communal latrine can be seen, built into the back of the rampart, while to the right, a series of circular ovens have been exposed. They were perhaps allocated one per barrack block, for the men to do their own cooking. (© Skyscan/Corbis)

A fragment of a bronze diploma (*RMD* 5, 332), issued in AD 90 to men in the auxiliary garrison of Judaea who had been honourably discharged after 25 years' service. The document guaranteed their citizenship and their right to contract a legal marriage. Although each diploma was personalized to the individual recipient, it typically listed all of the auxiliary units whose men were discharged on the same day. The names of two cavalry squadrons and seven infantry cohorts can be read, along with the name of the provincial governor, Titus Pomponius Bassus. (The Israel Museum, Jerusalem/ The Bridgeman Art Library)

Third Gallica, which remained part of the Syrian garrison throughout.

Roman citizens had traditionally served a maximum of 16 years in the legions, but mindful of the costs of demobilization – veterans were entitled to a substantial cash reward (probably equivalent to ten years' pay) and a place in a *colonia* ('veteran colony') as well as certain prerogatives such as exemption from taxation – Augustus increased this, first to 20 years, and finally to 25. (The Praetorians, on the other hand, were expected to serve only 16 years.) On enrolment, recruits took an oath to serve the emperor, and renewed it every year with much pomp and ceremony, so that their loyalty was clear. The severity of the army's discontent with Galba was demonstrated by the failure of the upper Rhine legions to renew their oath to him on 1 January AD 69; this signalled the emperor's loss of *auctoritas*.

New legions were raised only occasionally, because of the financial burden that this would entail. When Caligula enrolled two new legions for service on the Rhine, he chose to name them the Fifteenth Primigenia (the number was probably chosen to complement the Fourteenth Gemina and Sixteenth Gallica, stationed at Mogontiacum) and the Twenty-Second Primigenia (probably as a companion to the Twenty-First Rapax, stationed at Vetera). The next emperor to enrol a new legion was Nero, for his Caucasus campaign; he chose to name it the First Italica Legion, drawing attention to its Italian origin and beginning a new sequence that would wait 100 years to be continued.

Since before the days of Augustus, the legion had comprised ten *cohortes* ('cohorts'), each divided into six *centuriae* ('centuries'), with the exception of the first cohort, which (for reasons that are not yet clear) had only five. The entire legion was commanded by a senatorial *legatus* ('legate') assisted by six tribunes, all of whom held the post for only a few years. Continuity of command

was provided by the centurions, who were not bound by the service conditions of the common legionaries. Many served for a lifetime, attracted by the high level of pay and the prospects of advancement (if only for a select few). The most senior centurions were promoted into the first cohort, where they were known as the *primi ordines* (because they commanded the 'first ranks'); of these, the *primus pilus* ('chief centurion') served for only a single year before advancing to the highly respected post of *praefectus castrorum* ('prefect of the camp') or transferring into the equestrian service.

As soon as the legions became permanent fixtures, they required their own accommodation, tailored to military needs. Thus, it became common to station an entire legion – or even, in the 1st century, a pair of legions – inside a single fortress, built along the lines of a town, with a central headquarters building (taking the place of the town's forum) and a hospital and baths complex for the health and welfare of the men, as well as spacious housing for the well-to-do officers. The common legionaries were accommodated in long strip buildings, built facing one another in pairs across a grid of alleyways; each strip was a barracks for a complete *centuria* ('century') of 80-odd men, with a more generous allowance at one end for the centurion. The fortress itself was normally four-sided, defended by a high rampart and external ditch, and could only be entered through closely monitored gateways, set at (or near) the midpoint of each side.

Scene LVII on Trajan's Column, showing Roman legionaries engaged in construction work (left), beside the impaled heads of their barbarian enemies, while auxiliary infantry guard a wooden bridge (centre). Cavalry (perhaps the *equites singulares Augusti*) follow the bareheaded emperor Trajan (right).

The legions did not stand alone. The energies of Rome's *peregrini* ('non-citizens'), chiefly those from the more warlike parts of the empire (north-west Spain, for example, or Thrace), were channelled into the so-called *auxilia* ('auxiliary troops'), which assisted the legions, often by providing an alternative to the heavily armed infantry. 'Celtic' Europe provided a steady supply of horsemen, the Levant produced archers, and general-purpose infantry were raised all around the empire's perimeter. By the time of Claudius, it was common practice to organize these into separate cavalry squadrons (known as *alae*, 'wings') and infantry *cohortes* ('cohorts') of roughly 500 men. (The technical term *quingenaria* indicates '500-strong', but the basic building-blocks – *turmae* or 'troops' of 32 horsemen and *centuriae* or 'centuries' of 80 infantrymen – did not favour round hundreds.) A third type of unit, the *cohors equitata* or 'equitate cohort', was a hybrid of both, and comprised a cavalry element and an infantry element; these became by far the most numerous of the auxiliary units, no doubt on account of their in-built flexibility.

Like the legions, the auxiliary units were numbered, and their names preserved a record of their original recruiting area. A new sequence was begun with each recruitment drive, however, resulting in a preponderance of Firsts and Seconds and fewer larger numerals. The early garrison of Britannia gives a flavour of these, with names such as the First Squadron of Spanish Asturians and the First Squadron of Pannonians, or the eight cohorts of Batavians that accompanied the Fourteenth Gemina Legion to the Continent at Nero's behest. However, individual units were sent far and wide across the empire, and, although they retained their original names, their ethnic composition gradually changed as they began to recruit closer to their current station.

From the time of Claudius, upon their honourable discharge, auxiliaries were rewarded with Roman citizenship, not only for themselves but also for any children they may have fathered in the meantime.

(However, they were not permitted to marry during military service, so their existing partners remained *peregrinae*, 'foreigners'.) Individuals could prove their citizen rights by obtaining a bronze diptych conventionally known as a *diploma*. These official documents recorded the names of the veteran and his superior officer, along with a list of auxiliary units stationed in the same province, and from which men were also released on the same day.

Individual units were housed within their own forts, normally (it seems) singly, but occasionally brigaded with another unit; cavalry in particular might be billeted alongside a legion in its fortress, to give the commander maximum tactical flexibility. Like fortresses, these forts were defensive structures, but on a far less grand scale. For one thing, they normally covered less than a tenth of the area covered by a fortress; for another, the auxiliaries were not blessed with such a range of amenities. The headquarters building still sat at the centre; however, besides the commanding officer's house, and a pair of granaries to store a year's supply of foodstuffs, the fort contained only barrack blocks. A small baths building was often provided outside the ramparts.

The Roman officer class

The Roman army was commanded, at the highest level, by senators. Augustus had instituted a formal *cursus honorum* ('sequence of offices') for all senators to follow. At the age of 25, they were expected to gain election to one of the 20 posts as *quaestor* (a junior finance official) available each year. Prior to this, they will have indicated their intention of embarking on a senatorial career by serving in one of the four boards of minor magistrates (the so-called *vigintiviri*, or '20 men') at Rome. Many prospective senators also served for a limited period as a legionary tribune (known as the *tribunus laticlavius*, 'broad-striped tribune', in reference to the senator's hallmark purple stripe), but there were fewer than 30 openings, and candidates may have relied upon personal recommendation to secure one.

At the age of 30, senators were expected to fill one of the dozen annually available vacancies as *praetor* (a legal official). After their year of office, the *praetorii* ('men who had been praetor') could fulfil a number of functions *pro praetore* ('with praetorian status'). Thus, they supplied the governors for the less important imperial provinces, the so-called 'praetorian' provinces of Aquitania,

Belgica, Lugdunensis, Lusitania and Galatia (others were added later). As the emperor's delegate, they took the title of *legatus Augusti pro praetore* ('legate of Augustus with praetorian status') and served at the emperor's pleasure (in practice, three years or so). They were also eligible to govern eight of the ten senatorial provinces – the praetorian provinces of Achaia, Baetica, Bithynia et Pontus, Creta et Cyrenae, Macedonia, Narbonensis, Sardinia and Sicilia (Augustus had exchanged Narbonensis for Illyricum) – for which they were selected by lot for a one-year term. Confusingly, in this case, they were traditionally known as 'proconsuls'. The ex-praetor could also command a legion, taking the title *legatus legionis* ('legionary legate'); as these were, by and large, stationed in the imperial provinces, service was again at the emperor's pleasure.

A select few ex-praetors might proceed to the consulship, Rome's pre-eminent magistracy, at the age of 42. (Thus, the future emperor Vespasian, born in AD 9, became consul in AD 51.) Augustus arranged for the sons of well-connected patrician families to hold a consulship earlier, some even ten years earlier. (The emperor Galba, for example, born in 3 BC, was able to hold the consulship in AD 33, while his rival Vitellius, born in AD 15, held his in AD 48; it is a mystery why Trajan, born in AD 53, did not hold the consulship until AD 91, although his father had been granted patrician status.)

Originally, two consuls served as colleagues for a full year. However, only ex-consuls were eligible to govern the important 'consular' provinces (mostly those with large legionary armies), so gradually the custom arose of replacing the consular pair (known as the *consules ordinarii*,

The tombstone of Titus Calidius Severus (*ILS* 2596), who rose through the ranks to become a legionary centurion. Having been promoted to the legionary cavalry, he was then transferred into an auxiliary equitate cohort with the rank of decurion (officer in charge of a troop of 32 cavalrymen), before finally becoming a centurion in the Fifteenth Apollinaris Legion. He died at the age of 58, having served Rome for 34 years. (Matthias Kabel/CC-BY 2.5)

The emperor Hadrian's *adventus* ('arrival') in Rome, possibly returning from the Second Jewish War. He is surrounded by his fellow senators, and receives, from the goddess Roma (the warlike personification of Rome), an orb, symbolizing the Roman world. (De Agostini/Getty Images)

'ordinary consuls') partway through the year with so-called suffect consuls (from the Roman word *suffectus*, meaning 'substitute'). This practice ensured a sufficiently large pool of qualified candidates (and gave emperors the option of rewarding more men). It also explains how, for example, Publius Petronius Turpilianus and Lucius Caesennius Paetus, the ordinary consuls for AD 61, could each commence their consular governorship (of Britain and Cappadocia–Galatia respectively) in that same year. It was Roman practice to identify each year by the names of the *consules ordinarii*, which made the ordinary consulship a signal honour, especially when held with the emperor as colleague.

A number of posts were open to *consulares* ('men who had been consul'). Most prestigious of all was the *praefectus urbi* ('prefect of the city'), who combined legal powers with the overall command of the urban cohorts. Perhaps the next highest honour was selection as proconsul of Africa or Asia, the two plum senatorial provinces; these unique one-year governorships, bestowed at least five years (in practice, ten or so) after the consulship, usually marked the end of a man's senatorial career. However, before that occurred, ex-consuls played the important role of governing those provinces with large legionary armies: initially under Augustus, these were Illyricum, Syria, Tarraconensis and the two military zones on the Rhine (later called Germania Superior and Germania Inferior), but the frontier provinces of Pannonia and Moesia were soon added, and eventually Cappadocia. Like their praetorian counterparts, these consular governors also held the title of *legatus Augusti pro praetore* – since the emperor himself technically held the proconsular command, his deputies were only granted praetorian powers.

These were the high commands. It looks very much as if Augustus decided to employ *equites* ('knights'), members of Rome's equestrian order, in the lower military commands, chiefly in charge of the auxiliary units. Of course, the vast majority of equestrians probably held no military post at all, being content to wield municipal authority. But the concept of the *militia equestris* ('equestrian military service') gradually developed, as equestrians increasingly served as *praefectus equitum*

('cavalry prefect') or, as the post gradually came to be known, *praefectus alae* ('prefect of a cavalry squadron'), often preceded by a stint as *praefectus cohortis* ('prefect of an infantry cohort'). The third army post reserved for equestrians was the military tribunate. We have seen that the aspiring senator, barely out of his teens, might begin his career as a tribune in one of the emperor's legions, but each legion traditionally had six tribunes; the other five posts were filled by *equites*, often designated *tribuni angusticlavii* ('narrow-stripe tribunes'), to draw a distinction with the *tribunus laticlavius*. These posts, like the senatorial commands, are thought to have averaged three years' duration.

Unlike the senatorial *cursus honorum*, there was no uniform age for entry into the *militia equestris*. Some officers were young men from privileged families; others were legionary veterans and, by implication, more advanced in years. For example, Marcus Valerius Speratus, a veteran of the Seventh Claudia Legion, achieved a promoted post on the Moesian governor's staff, which (no doubt through the workings of patronage) gave him access to an equestrian career, for he went on to command the First Aquitanian Cohort in Britain, where he died aged 55 (*ILS* 7173).

By the reign of Claudius, the equestrian career had settled into a standard sequence of *tres militiae* ('three military posts', later joined by a fourth, when the development of a new enlarged cavalry squadron necessitated the creation of a senior commander), but many men were content to serve only as legionary tribune before retiring to municipal life. Others, a select few with the right patronage, having survived each stage, might progress to a junior administrative post, such as one of the finance officers and secretaries in the imperial 'civil service'. Alternatively, men who had completed their *tres militiae* might progress to one of the fiscal procuratorships, handling the payment and supply of the army in the imperial provinces, or a praesidial procuratorship, as governor of one of the smaller provinces (notably Noricum and Raetia). Prior to the

Scene XL on Trajan's Column, showing Roman soldiers (bottom register) in battle against the Dacians (top register). The legionaries are differentiated from the auxiliaries by their characteristic banded armour (the so-called *lorica segmentata*). A group of legionaries are in charge of mobile artillery (top left), while an auxiliary soldier brings a prisoner to the emperor Trajan (bottom left).

reign of Claudius, these posts had been held by equestrian *praefecti* ('prefects').

As in the senatorial career, there were a host of non-military posts and functions that might intervene along the way, and the system did not reach full maturity until the 2nd century. However, throughout the Principate, at the pinnacle of the equestrian career sat the three great prefectures at Rome – the post of *praefectus annonae* ('prefect of the corn supply') and the commands of the *vigiles* and the *praetoriani* – and the prestigious *praefectura Aegypti* ('prefecture of Egypt').

Simultaneously, a meritocratic system evolved, whereby the professional soldiers of the legions (like Valerius Speratus, mentioned earlier) might aspire to greater things. A key role was played by the legionary centurions, who were usually long-service officers who had risen *ex caliga* ('from the infantry ranks') with 15 or so years under their belts. For example, Quintus Etuvius Capreolus spent 14 years in the Fourth Scythica Legion, ten of them in a promoted post, before becoming centurion; he served in that post for 21 years before achieving equestrian status, and then commanded the Second Thracian

Cohort for five years, finally dying at the age of 60 (*ILS* 9090).

Some legionary centurions were men who had been honourably discharged from the Praetorian Guard after their 16-year stint. Of course, a little patronage always helped, as in the case of Marcus Vettius Valens (*ILS* 2648), who managed to be at the right place at the right time. Having enlisted as a *praetorianus* around AD 28, he accompanied Claudius to Britain as assistant to the emperor's *praefectus praetorio* Rufrius Pollio; while Claudius' higher-ranking companions received honours, Valens was 'decorated with torques, armlets and *phalerae*', an enviable set of *dona militaria* ('military decorations'). By then, he had almost served his time, but elected to stay on as an *evocatus* (a veteran who has been 'called back' into service, usually on account of some special skill). He was promptly promoted to a round of centurionates at Rome (far more prestigious than an ordinary legionary posting) in the various security forces known as the *vigiles*, *statores*, *urbaniciani* and *speculatores*, before finally returning to the *praetoriani*. Such a successful career qualified Valens for the one-year post of legionary *primus pilus* (the 'chief centurion'), which was the traditional jumping-off point for transition to an equestrian career. However, Valens' particular skills led him back to Rome, where he obtained a round of tribunates (in the *vigiles*, *urbaniciani* and *praetoriani*) before achieving the equestrian procuratorship of Lusitania in AD 66.

The Roman fort of Cilurnum (present-day Chesters) on Hadrian's Wall, viewed from the north, showing the typical rectangular 'playing card' shape. The fort was designed to accommodate a 500-strong cavalry squadron. The ends of two barrack blocks can be seen in the north-east quadrant (left). Each double cubicle is thought to have accommodated three men and their mounts, with the horses stabled in the outer cubicle. The headquarters building can be seen in its usual position in the centre of the fort, and alongside it to the east lie the remains of the commander's house, which was roughly the size of two barrack blocks. (© Skyscan/Corbis)

Other centurions were equestrians who had elected to follow this route in preference to the standard *militia equestris*. Naturally, their privileged background gave them an in-built advantage and perhaps guaranteed a certain level of promotion. The tombstone of Tiberius Claudius Vitalis advertises the fact that he joined the centurionate *ex equite Romano* ('from the Roman equestrian order') and, over the course of 11 years, was

promoted in succession from the Fifth Macedonica Legion to the First Italica Legion ... from the First Italica Legion to the First Minervia Legion ... from the First Minervia Legion to the Twentieth Valeria Victrix Legion, likewise promoted in the same legion, and promoted in

succession from the Twentieth Valeria Victrix Legion to the Ninth Hispana Legion ... from the Ninth Hispana Legion to the Seventh Claudia Legion, likewise promoted in the same legion ... (ILS 2656)

He died aged 41 as the fourth most senior centurion of the legion, having been decorated twice for service in Dacia.

All of these officers were paid a salary. The proconsuls of Asia and Africa received a one-off payment of one million sesterces; the consular legates perhaps expected something in the order of 500,000 sesterces per year; top-grade equestrian procurators were paid 200,000 sesterces; and legionary commanders probably 150,000 sesterces. The *praefectus alae* perhaps received 50,000 sesterces, the tribune 25,000, and the *praefectus cohortis* half as much again. The legionary centurion, on the other hand, earned only 13,500 sesterces (in the 1st century), but this was around 15 times the normal legionary's pay. The centurions of the first cohort (the so-called *primi ordines*) probably received double this amount, and the *primus pilus*, for his one-year stint, received quadruple.

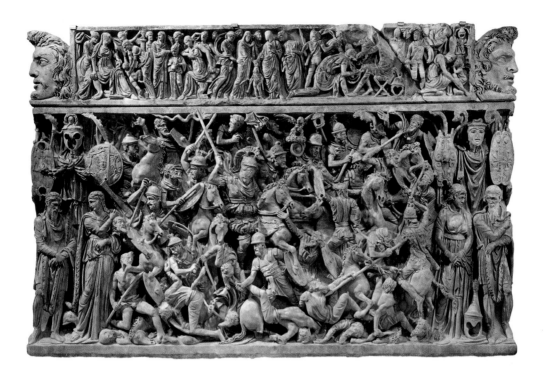

Battle scene on the Portonaccio sarcophagus, depicted in the characteristic high relief technique of the Antonine era. A victory trophy can be seen at either side, above the figures of barbarian captives, representing Dacians (left) and Suebian Germans (right). Along the lid (top), a procession of Roman clients queue to greet their seated patron, the unknown occupant of the sarcophagus. Behind him, soldiers guard more barbarian prisoners beneath another victory trophy. (De Agostini/Getty Images)

The northern barbarians

Across the northern frontiers lay lands occupied by an array of tribal groupings, some of which had struck agreements of friendship with Rome. Across the lower Rhine, the tribes of the Batavi ('Batavians') and Frisii had entered into treaty relations, the former promising military service, the latter promising supplies, but the Chauci along the North Sea coast and the Bructeri opposite Castra Vetera (the 'old camp' at present-day Xanten) were more troublesome. Likewise, along the upper Rhine, the tribe of the Chatti (from whom, ironically, the loyal Batavi had sprung) provided more than one Roman general with an excuse for campaigning. Tacitus famously remarked that 'you would see other peoples going to battle, but the Chatti wage war' (*On Germany* 30.3). Further into the interior, the powerful tribe of the Cherusci, who had skilfully engineered the *clades Variana*, gradually burnt themselves out in internal squabbling. However, even they respected the might of Rome; in AD 47, they applied to Claudius to grant them a new king, in much the same way that the Armenians on the eastern frontier were expected to behave.

By and large, these societies shared some of Rome's values. The maintenance of an upper class through the acquisition of martial glory and the control of luxury items meant that they were often eager to interact with the Roman empire, even to the extent of serving in her armed forces. Furthermore, respect for the system of patronage meant that the Roman emperor could manipulate their internal politics by insisting upon authorizing the tribes' choice of kings. All of this created a certain equilibrium along the river frontier; any trouble by and large manifested itself not as a 'barbarian invasion', but as disruption of the frontier zone.

A Roman legionary attacks a Dacian family, travelling with their four-wheeled wagon, on one of the metopes from the Tropaeum Traiani. The man wears the *pilleum* felt cap and carries the lethal two-handed curved blade (the so-called *falx*), which are the characteristics of the Dacian warrior. His wife pleads for mercy, while their child flees in terror. (CristianChirita/CC-BY-SA-3.0)

Beyond the Black Forest and the (largely vacant) re-entrant angle of the upper Rhine that the Romans called the *agri decumates* ('tithe lands') lay the two large Suebian tribes of the Marcomanni and the Quadi, occupying modern Bohemia and Slovakia,

north of the upper Danube. Transdanubian relations here were generally friendly. At the time of the *clades Variana*, the Marcomannic king, Maroboduus, had refused to support the Cherusci and, as a result, had won Roman friendship. Tiberius gave him refuge when he was ousted in AD 17, and appointed a new king with sovereignty over both tribes, who lasted well into the reign of Nero. Although these tribes appear never to have paid tribute to Rome, traders moved to and fro with impunity.

Downriver, the newly arrived Sarmatian tribes, migrating westwards and roaming the plains, were more changeable in their loyalties. These were the Jazyges of the Hungarian plain, squeezed (with Roman permission) between the border of Pannonia and the lands of Dacia, and the Roxolani of the Danube estuary, rubbing shoulders with the Germanic Bastarnae. In between, ringed by the Carpathian Mountains, lay the kingdom of Dacia (Transylvania in present-day Romania), which had quickly outstripped its neighbours in sophistication, owing to its mineral-rich country.

Unlike their Germanic and Sarmatian neighbours, the Dacian aristocratic society had reached a stage of urbanization, with a centralized royal capital at Sarmizegethusa Regia. Their towns, tucked away in the heart of the Orastie Mountains, were massively fortified using the so-called *murus Dacicus* technique (stone-faced ramparts with timber-laced rubble filling), and cleverly utilized the hilly landscape in their defences, while outlying towers covered the approaches. However, just like the Germans and Sarmatians, the Dacians classified warfare as a glorious pursuit, and had managed to evolve a sophisticated military organization, partly by exploiting Greek and Roman knowledge. Their rich resources fuelled a developing culture that could easily threaten Roman hegemony over the Balkans, and the 1st-century Roman governors of Moesia must have viewed their Dacian neighbours with some unease.

The Parthians

In the east, Rome found an enemy with resources equal to her own: the Parthian empire. Actually a confederation of Iranian peoples, only the Parthian empire's western Mesopotamian province, ruled from the capital at Ctesiphon (near modern Baghdad in Iraq), made any impact on Roman consciousness, and then only because of the threat it posed to Roman Syria. The Romans were always mindful of the humiliating reverses that had been suffered by Roman armies in Parthian territory (chiefly, but not only, Crassus at Carrhae in 53 BC), but their ambitions were limited to Mesopotamia, and they never came close to threatening the Parthian heartland.

Indeed, the peace treaty concluded with Parthia in 20 BC was represented by Augustus as a Roman victory, since he had received back the legionary battle-standards captured from Crassus at Carrhae, along with Parthian 'hostages' and the promise that Armenia should remain neutral. The agreement was respected by both sides for over a century, by and large, although each generation of Parthians tested the Roman resolve.

The Romans of the Principate were fortunate to find a Parthian nobility distracted by affairs elsewhere in their empire, unlike their 3rd-century successors, who were forced to tackle the more belligerent Sassanian kings. The Parthians of the 1st century may have dreamed of ruling Syria and Anatolia, as their Persian forebears had done, but they made no effort to make the dream a reality. The fertile plains of lower Mesopotamia were sufficient. Parthia's hold on northern Mesopotamia was less sure – the cities of Edessa and Hatra operated as independent states – but, as long as the Romans respected the upper Euphrates as a border and refrained from annexing the Armenian kingdom outright, the Parthian king had no particular reason to pick a quarrel.

An uneasy peace

Wrestling with the wolf

The death of Augustus gave the Principate its first test. Could a new, less charismatic leader, who patently lacked the first emperor's *auctoritas*, nevertheless exert imperial authority over his fellow senators and project that authority beyond the frontiers? The new reign opened with crisis in the north and in Africa, and it would close with crisis in the east, an early indicator of how fragile the much-vaunted *pax Romana* really was.

Tiberius (aged 55 on his accession) was apparently fond of using a Greek proverb to describe the predicament in which he reluctantly found himself: 'he often declared that he was holding the wolf by the ears' (Suetonius, *Life of Tiberius* 25.1), meaning that he couldn't keep holding on, and yet he dare not let go. One source of disquiet was certainly Augustus' new professional army. On receiving news of their emperor's death, mutiny had broken out among the legions in Illyricum and along the Rhine; perhaps assuming that their allegiance was to Augustus personally, they did not know what to expect under a new emperor.

Some time after the *clades Variana*, the northern military command had been divided into an *exercitus Germanicus superior* ('upper German army') and an *exercitus Germanicus inferior* ('lower German army'), conveniently maintaining the fiction that Rome controlled German territory. In AD 14, the two armies, each numbering four legions, were commanded by Aulus Caecina Severus in the north and Gaius Silius Largus in the south. In Illyricum, the three legions fell under the command of Quintus Junius Blaesus and Publius Cornelius Dolabella. All four men transferred their loyalty to Tiberius without question; the commander of the other great concentration of legions,

in Spain, was Marcus Aemilius Lepidus, another loyal servant. Indeed, Tiberius was well thought of in military circles, having campaigned successfully on the northern frontier during the reign of Augustus and having merited two triumphs, celebrated in 7 BC and AD 12.

Just prior to his death, Augustus had sent his grandson Germanicus to take overall command on the Rhine, and had apparently intended to send Tiberius to Illyricum; instead, Tiberius sent his son, Drusus, in the care of his Praetorian Prefect, the ambitious Lucius Aelius Sejanus. Both young men succeeded in defusing the situation in

The emperor Tiberius was particularly revered by the *praetoriani*, who appear to have taken his scorpion emblem (his birth sign was Scorpio) as their own. (Leemage/Getty Images)

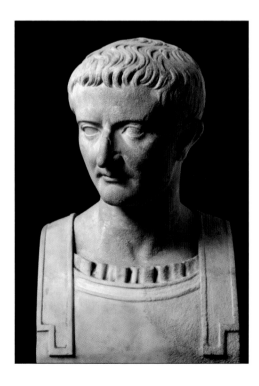

their respective provinces – Germanicus, with the two-year-old Caligula at his side, played on the men's sentimentality (from his trademark miniature military boots, Caligula was something of a mascot to the northern armies), while Drusus made opportune use of a timely eclipse to exploit the men's superstition – but the situation had revealed the inherent dangers of a state that relied on military power.

In the aftermath, Germanicus was given free rein to restore Roman prestige beyond the Rhine, expunging the disgrace of the *clades Variana*. During two campaigning seasons, he utilized the age-old invasion route from Castra Vetera, heading east along the River Lippe into the lands of the Cherusci, and finally brought the tribes to battle at Idistaviso (in an unknown location that Tacitus, *Annals* 2.16, places 'between the [River] Weser and the hills'). Two of the three eagle standards lost by Varus were recovered, and Germanicus was recalled to celebrate a triumph in AD 17 (his deputies, Caecina and Silius, received *ornamenta triumphalia*), indicating that Tiberius had no serious plans for the annexation of Germania Magna. In this, he was following Augustus' admonition to maintain the empire within its boundaries.

Meanwhile, in AD 14, the governor of Africa proconsularis, Lucius Nonius Asprenas, was putting the final touches to a 'fortified road from the winter camp to Tacape' (*ILS* 151). The road-builders were the Third Augusta Legion, the last legion to remain under the control of a senatorial governor. Their 'winter camp' probably lay at Ammaedara, present-day Haidra in Tunisia (their famous legionary fortress at Lambaesis in Numidia wasn't built until the reign of Trajan). The road they built, running 200 miles south-east to the coast, carved through the lands of the Musulamii.

Rome had experienced previous trouble with this powerful Gaetulian tribe, most recently in AD 6, when Cossus Cornelius Lentulus won *ornamenta triumphalia* for success in a 'Gaetulian war' (*AE* 1940, 68). A generation or so earlier, Augustus had installed Juba II as the 'friendly king' of Mauretania, a fiefdom that sprawled across modern Morocco and northern Algeria, and had planted a dozen veteran colonies there. This had caused ructions among the indigenous nomadic peoples, who were accustomed to wandering as far afield as modern Libya, and gave Roman generals the opportunity to score victories – most famously, Lucius Cornelius Balbus in 19 BC, the last 'ordinary citizen' to celebrate a full triumph.

Cossus' war clearly hadn't solved the problem. In AD 17, a Romanized Musulamian chieftain named Tacfarinas began a seven-year guerrilla campaign against the Roman assets in the province. According to the historian Tacitus, he had succeeded in organizing his rag-tag followers 'in the military style, by detachments and troops' (Tacitus, *Annals* 2.52). An initial Roman victory

A northern barbarian, thought to be a representative of one of the Sarmatian tribes, depicted on a metope from the later (AD 108) Tropaeum Traiani at Adamklissi. (CristianChirita/CC-BY-SA-3.0)

earned the proconsul Marcus Furius Camillus *ornamenta triumphalia*, but his successor, Lucius Apronius, proved less effective against Tacfarinas' hit-and-run tactics, succeeding only in increasing the rebel's arrogance.

By AD 21, Tiberius had decided that serious action was required. Africa was too important to the Roman economy to allow Tacfarinas' disturbance to continue. (Cicero, *On Pompey's Command* 34, called Africa one of the 'three corn reserves of the Roman Republic', along with Sicily and Sardinia; and even after Augustus' annexation of Egypt delivered the bounty of the fertile Nile valley to Rome, Africa remained a major food supplier.) Instead of allowing the senate to select the governor, as was usual for this province, the emperor directed Quintus Junius Blaesus – who was the uncle of the powerful Sejanus – to lay down his Pannonian command and travel to Africa with one of his legions, the Ninth Hispana (whose current commander bore the historic name of Publius Cornelius Scipio – an honorific inscription gives him the grand title of *legatus Tiberi Caesaris Augusti legionis VIIII Hispanae*, 'Tiberius Caesar Augustus' legate of the Ninth Hispana Legion': *ILS* 940).

Blaesus (characterized by Tacitus as 'experienced in military affairs, with a robust constitution, and competent in warfare'; *Annals* 3.32) divided his two-legion army into roving units under the command of proven centurions and, for two years, harried Tacfarinas all year round, using the rebel's own tactics against him. When Blaesus' troops hailed their successful general as *imperator*, Tiberius – a man who studiously avoided the title that Augustus had taken as his own – permitted it (though, from then on, this would be yet another military honour that the emperors denied to others). Blaesus returned to Rome and the expected award of *ornamenta triumphalia*, while the Ninth Hispana Legion returned to Pannonia. Yet Tacfarinas was still at large.

Meanwhile, the accession of Juba's son, Ptolemy, as ruler in Mauretania caused an exodus of Moorish troops to Tacfarinas' side, where they were joined by Garamantian tribesmen and disaffected provincials. As things grew worse, the new governor of Africa, Publius Cornelius Dolabella, pooled his military resources with Ptolemy's and continued the tactics that had won Blaesus such success. Tacfarinas' forces were finally surprised near Auzea (thought to be near present-day Sour El-Ghozlane, in Algeria) and the rebel leader was killed. When Dolabella applied for *ornamenta triumphalia*, the contrary emperor refused (not wishing to detract from Sejanus' uncle's glory). Nevertheless, it was Dolabella's name that became associated with the defeat of Tacfarinas, and he erected at least one dedication to *Victoria Augusta* ('The emperor's victory', a kind of imperial patron deity), 'on account of Tacfarinas having been slain' (*AE* 1961, 107). Despite Augustus' admonition, an almost imperceptible side effect of seven years of desultory warfare had been to increase the area of the Roman province at the expense of tribal lands.

Back in Gaul, where the Roman authorities had recently conducted a census, the provinces of Lugdunensis and Belgica were stirred into rebellion by two men named Julius Florus and Julius Sacrovir, outraged by the heavy level of taxation. (Perhaps learning from this event, Tiberius later advised one of his governors that 'I want my sheep shorn, not shaved', according to Cassius Dio, *Roman History* 57.10.5.) The rebels tried, unsuccessfully, to win over a Roman cavalry squadron – such units being, at this stage, largely composed of Gallic natives commanded by their own chieftains – but the trouble was quelled by Silius, the commander on the upper Rhine, whose legionary troops were briefly delayed by the Gallic gladiators fighting on Sacrovir's side. (In a colourful passage, Tacitus, *Annals* 3.46, explains that 'the iron-clad [gladiators] caused a brief delay, as their laminated armour was resistant to javelins and swords, but the soldiers snatched up their axes and picks, and cut through the bodies and their protection, as if they were breaking through a wall'.)

Some years later, in AD 28, another revolt broke out, this time among the Frisii, the tribe who lived across the Rhine delta, along the North Sea coast. Here was another nation who were, strictly speaking, outside the Roman empire, but who paid tribute as a mark of their loyalty. In this case, the tribute consisted of ox hides, which an overzealous official had lately decided were too small, justifying the extortion of other forms of taxation. The tribal response was violent, and the garrison of a fort called Flevum (probably Velsen in the Netherlands) was

besieged for a time (archaeology has revealed the barrage of sling bullets directed at the occupants). The commander of the lower Rhine army, Lucius Apronius (a veteran of Germanicus' campaigns across the Rhine and a previous proconsul of Africa), succeeded in drawing the besiegers away with an assault on their homeland, but in the process

The *Grand Camée de France* depicts Tiberius in the guise of Jupiter, seated beside his mother (Augustus' wife) Livia. The deified Augustus floats above, flanked by the deceased Drusus and Germanicus, while the armour-clad child (centre left) represents Caligula. The Parthian captive perhaps alludes to the diplomatic victory of AD 35. (Marie-Lan Nguyen/CC-BY-2.5)

suffered an enormous defeat, which Tiberius chose to ignore.

Changes occurred in the east also. Here, there were far more of these nations that Augustus had left in the hands of 'friendly and allied kings' (sometimes called in the Greek language of the east *philorhomaei*, 'friends of Rome'), while quite clearly considering them integral parts of the Roman empire (according to Suetonius, *Life of the Deified Augustus* 48, 'he treated them all as divisions and regions of the empire'). Provided their kings paid court to the emperor, which often meant sending their offspring to Rome to be educated in the Roman manner, they could continue to rule. One who failed to pay due honour to Tiberius was Archelaus of Cappadocia, whose wealthy kingdom, in the words of Tacitus, was 'reduced to a province' (*Annals* 2.42) in AD 17 and placed under the control of an equestrian prefect.

Although there had been warfare on the northern frontier and in Africa, diplomacy was preferred in the east, where Germanicus was sent to renew Augustus' non-aggression pact with Parthia. Part of this settlement guaranteed that any regime change in Armenia – a kingdom in which the Parthians took a particular interest, as it controlled the northern route into Mesopotamia – must be ratified by Rome. However, in AD 17, the Parthian king, Artabanus II, attempted to place his own brother on the throne in Artaxata. Affairs were resolved amicably with the crowning of a Roman nominee, but the Parthian king must have viewed with apprehension the new Roman province of Cappadocia, which brought the Roman empire right up to the Armenian border.

The eastern frontier remained quiet until AD 35, when the Armenian throne again fell vacant, and King Artabanus again attempted to install a relative, this time his son. The Roman governor of Syria, Lucius Vitellius (parent of the future short-lived emperor Vitellius) overawed him with a show of force, and even managed to secure Artabanus' sons as 'guests' at Rome. War in the east was once more averted, for the time being.

Extending the empire

Paranoia and fear

Following Augustus' dynastic principle, Tiberius (aged 78 at his death) left his grandson Gemellus as co-heir with Germanicus' son, Caligula; but the one soon eliminated the other, leaving Caligula in charge. His short reign has been characterized as chaotic and irresponsible, and it is possible that the emperor was psychotic. The biographer Suetonius claimed that he often quoted the phrase 'Let them hate me, as long as they fear me' (*Life of Caligula* 30.1). Nonetheless, modern historians frequently attempt to rehabilitate him by attempting to find logic behind his erratic behaviour.

One unfortunate precedent set by Caligula was the granting of an accession bonus to the Praetorian Guard – each man received 1,000 sesterces, which was more than the average legionary earned in a year. In fact, this was money that Tiberius had left in his will to the *praetoriani*, which the new emperor misrepresented as his own gift.

It is difficult to avoid the conclusion that Caligula's frontier policy was driven by whim. In the east, the tiny kingdom of Commagene, which Tiberius had attached to northern Syria, was restored to its last surviving prince, along with reparations for the years of Roman rule (it would finally be annexed by Vespasian), and Caligula's friend Herod Agrippa was granted an independent kingdom within the boundaries of the province of Judaea, which cannot have made the equestrian prefect's job any easier. In north Africa, King Ptolemy of Mauretania was executed for some imagined slight, and his huge kingdom was confiscated – not without incident, for Marcus Licinius Crassus Frugi seems to have earned *ornamenta triumphalia* for action in Mauretania at about this time.

Caligula was evidently paranoid. When Lucius Calpurnius Piso (the son of Germanicus' alleged murderer) became governor of Africa proconsularis in AD 39, the emperor (suspecting him of disloyalty) removed the Third Augusta Legion from his command; from then on, this legion was assigned to an imperial legate, like all the other legions. In the same year, Caligula executed the commander on the upper Rhine, Gnaeus Cornelius Lentulus Gaetulicus, for alleged involvement in a conspiracy.

Having rushed from Rome to Germany with his Praetorian Guard, he replaced Gaetulicus with the stern disciplinarian Servius Sulpicius Galba (himself a future emperor), and immediately staged military manoeuvres to whip the men into shape. The new commander was careful not to cross the suspicious emperor, and despite his 41 years 'even jogged along for 20 miles beside the emperor's chariot' (Suetonius, *Life of Galba* 6.3).

Caligula's eccentricity makes it difficult to assess whether the manoeuvres were a serious prelude to an invasion of Britain. On the one hand, two new legions – the Fifteenth Primigenia and Twenty-Second Primigenia – were created at around this time, increasing the number of Rhine legions to ten and the total empire-wide complement to 27. Whenever later emperors raised new legions (admittedly a rare event), it signalled that campaigning was in the offing, with the possibility of annexing new territory. It certainly seems that a British prince, Adminius, had fled to Caligula's court from the clutches of his father, Cunobelinus (king of the Catuvellauni, occupying present-day Hertfordshire and Essex), so a valid *casus belli* was available. On the other hand, later historians' allegations that the emperor set his troops to collecting sea-shells on the North Sea coast may (if true) indicate that Caligula envisaged a struggle against the Ocean, the mighty deity who encircled the known world and whose untamed power would prey upon the minds of Claudius' soldiers some years later. The construction of a lighthouse at Gesoriacum (modern Boulogne) in AD 40 could fit either scenario.

A wise fool

Eventually, Caligula's bizarre behaviour exasperated even his loyal Praetorian Guard, who abruptly assassinated him and foisted his lame, stuttering, bookish uncle Claudius (who was by then 50 years old) upon the senate as the next emperor. This was not exactly how Augustus' dynastic principle was supposed to work, but nobody wished to argue with the *praetoriani*. Claudius immediately added the names 'Caesar Augustus' to his own to bolster his legitimacy, and set about acquiring the military credentials that he conspicuously lacked (Claudius had never even embarked upon a senatorial career, far less commanded an army).

Fortunately, that same year, campaigning by the newly enlarged armies of the Rhine against the Chatti and Chauci of the north – which must have begun under Caligula, who perhaps had delusions of emulating the German campaigns of his father, Germanicus – came to a successful conclusion, and resulted in the recovery of the third and last eagle standard lost in the *clades Variana*. These exploits earned Galba and his colleague, Publius Gabinius Secundus, *ornamenta triumphalia* and enabled the

Imaginative view of the Forum Romanum as it might have appeared under the emperor Septimius Severus, after the two centuries of imperial Roman warfare covered in this book. Severus' massive triumphal arch occupies the centre foreground, and to the right is the portico of the Temple of Vespasian and Titus, erected in the AD 80s by the emperor Domitian. In the background (and larger than life) looms the Flavian amphitheatre, nowadays known as the Colosseum. The hill to the right is the Palatine, where the emperors had their palaces. (The free-standing Column of Phocas, in the centre, is an obvious anachronism, having been erected in AD 608.) (Bridgeman/Getty)

unmilitary emperor to be hailed as *imperator*, though he never used the title as one of his names in the way that Augustus had.

There was trouble, too, in Mauretania, whose king had been suddenly removed by Caligula. Claudius was obliged to send two generals in succession, Gaius Suetonius Paullinus, who campaigned in the high Atlas Mountains and was, in fact, the first Roman to cross over to the Sahara, and Gnaeus Hosidius Geta, who scored two victories against the Moorish rebels. (No *ornamenta triumphalia* are mentioned, but the campaigns were probably overshadowed by the preparations for a far grander expedition on the other side of the Mediterranean world.) Claudius subsequently reorganized the enormous kingdom into two provinces, to be governed by equestrians.

Claudius' unexpected accession was not universally welcomed. In AD 42, the governor of Dalmatia, Lucius Arruntius Camillus Scribonianus, attempted to raise a rebellion with the support of a few senatorial colleagues and the backing of his two-legion army. However, the superstitious soldiers had a change of heart when their legionary battle-standards allegedly 'refused' to be moved from their fortresses, and Claudius rewarded the two legions – hitherto known simply as the Seventh and the Eleventh – with the title 'Claudia'. Lucius Salvius Otho (father of the future emperor Otho) was sent to replace Scribonianus, who had either been lynched or had committed suicide.

The main event from the reign of Claudius was the expansion of the empire beyond the encircling ocean to embrace the British Isles. It is quite likely that, since the days of Augustus, the kingdoms of south-eastern Britain had maintained links with Rome, and perhaps enjoyed the same friendly relations as, for example, Thrace or (until recently) Mauretania. At any rate, chieftains of the Britons were known to have made offerings on the Capitol, a sure sign that they respected Roman hegemony, despite the fact that their country was (in the words of Vergil, *Eclogues* 1.66) 'totally cut off from the whole world'. The creation of a province there would be

a major coup. And, again, there was a valid excuse, this time in the person of Verica, a British refugee who petitioned Claudius to reinstate him as king of the Atrebates (the tribe occupying present-day Hampshire).

The army for the *expeditio Britannica* ('British expedition') comprised four legions – the Second Augusta, Fourteenth Gemina and Twentieth (later named Valeria Victrix) from the Rhineland, and the Ninth Hispana from Pannonia – accompanied by an unknown number of auxiliary units; Claudius placed it under the command of Aulus Plautius, who was summoned from the governorship of Pannonia. It seems that the soldiers, overawed by the power of the Ocean, were initially unwilling to embark on the enterprise, but were finally persuaded, and 'within a few days, the submission of

The emperor Claudius, depicted in heroic style as the supreme god Jupiter, with the eagle as symbol of imperial power. He wears the oak-leaf crown (*corona civica*), a favourite accessory of his, as it symbolized the saving of citizens' lives. Both hands have been restored, and may not originally have held the items depicted here. (Giovanni Dall'Orto)

part of the island was received, without battle or bloodshed' (Suetonius, *Life of the Deified Claudius* 17.2). It seems that, just like the friendly kingdom of Cappadocia in AD 17, south-eastern Britain was peacefully absorbed into the empire. Once beyond the modern boundaries of Kent, however, Plautius met stern resistance, but won a major engagement with the Catuvellaunian tribe, now led by Cunobelinus' sons, one of whom, Caratacus, fled the field to continue the struggle at a later date.

Plautius had been under strict instructions to summon the emperor for the final victory. Claudius left Rome in the care of Lucius Vitellius (a particular favourite – he had already been honoured by Claudius not only with a second ordinary consulship, but as the emperor's colleague in the consulship of AD 43) and travelled to Britain with a considerable entourage. The nervous emperor was always surrounded by a large bodyguard, which this time included elephants! Having witnessed the capture of Camulodunum (Colchester in Essex), the imperial party returned to Rome, leaving instructions for Plautius 'to subjugate the rest' (Cassius Dio, *Roman History* 60.21.5). With their sketchy geographical knowledge and limited opportunity for exploration at this stage, the Romans clearly underestimated the size of Britain.

Claudius celebrated his British triumph in AD 44 with a grand procession through Rome – the first in a generation – and a cash handout to the city populace. All the senators who had taken part in the invasion – either accompanying the emperor, like Plautius' kinsman Tiberius Plautius Silvanus Aelianus, or commanding the legions, like Titus Flavius Vespasianus (the future emperor Vespasian), his brother Titus Flavius Sabinus, and Gnaeus Hosidius Geta's brother, Gaius – were rewarded with *ornamenta triumphalia*, while Plautius received the unique honour of an *ovatio* (the lesser type of triumph, known as an 'ovation'), and Vitellius received the rare honour of a third consulship (again, as the emperor's colleague). A new issue of coinage in the

following year carried, on the reverse, the legend DE BRITANN (announcing Claudius' victory *de Britannis*, 'over the Britons').

Claudius was rather profligate with triumphal honours. In AD 47, Quintus Curtius Rufus received *ornamenta triumphalia* for employing the legions of the upper Rhine in excavating a silver mine, to the dismay of the exhausted soldiers, who saw their comrades on the lower Rhine pursuing glorious warfare under their 'old school' commander, Gnaeus Domitius Corbulo. The tribe of the Chauci had raided imperial territory and Corbulo chased them back, in the process cowing the Frisii, who (astonishingly) had remained fractious since their defeat of Apronius nearly 20 years earlier. Campaigning was cut short, however, by a cautious emperor, who ordered Corbulo back across the Rhine. The bitter pill was sweetened with the award of *ornamenta triumphalia*. Rufus' successor as commander on the upper Rhine, Publius Pomponius Secundus (one of Corbulo's half-brothers), was obliged to take action against the Chatti and, in the process, managed to liberate some survivors of the *clades Variana* who had been captives for 40 years! He, too, received *ornamenta triumphalia*.

Claudius made sure to reward himself, too. Having received his second imperatorial acclamation in AD 41 for the successes of Galba and Gabinius in Germany (his first, like Caligula's, had been taken on his accession), he rapidly accumulated honours until, by AD 46, he was advertising himself on the coinage as IMP XI (meaning 'having been acclaimed *imperator* 11 times'). The historian Cassius Dio thought that this was very bad form, as several of these acclamations had been occasioned by the British victory, whereas 'nobody should receive this title more than once during the same war' (*Roman History* 60.21.5). By the end of his reign, Claudius had managed to accumulate a staggering 27, far more than any other emperor.

Although the ancient historians treated Claudius as a fool, it is quite clear that, on his accession, he began a wide-ranging series of reforms. Like Augustus, he made sure to meet the needs of the populace at Rome with the likes of an upgraded water supply and a more secure grain supply. Other reforms were more overtly military. The formal organization of Rome's auxiliary forces into regular units commanded by members of the equestrian order was perhaps due to Claudius, and it is only from his reign that we start to find the so-called *diploma*s – bronze diptychs, officially engraved with proof of an auxiliary veteran's honourable discharge and the all-important grant of citizenship to the man and his offspring.

Provinces were reorganized as well. Mauretania has been mentioned already. In AD 43, Quintus Veranius (the recipient of a work by Onasander entitled *The General*) was sent to annex Lycia, a confederation of cities in Asia Minor where civil unrest had caused Roman casualties. Inscriptions show that Veranius governed the new province for a five-year term, bringing order (and an improved road network) with the assistance of troops seconded, probably, from Syria. In AD 44, the death of Herod Agrippa entailed the reorganization of Judaea as one of Claudius' new procuratorial provinces (the equestrian governors were henceforth styled 'procurators' instead of prefects). The first governor was the pro-Roman Alexandrian Jew Tiberius Julius Alexander, but his successors in the post were relatively insignificant members of the equestrian order. Claudius sent equestrian procurators to govern Raetia and Noricum as well.

Another 'friendly kingdom' lying, like Lycia and Judaea, within the empire was Thrace, whose inhabitants were divided between the mountain-people of the west and the pastoralists of the east, so that trouble had occasionally flared up requiring Roman intervention. To address the general instability of the region, Tiberius had created a super-province covering the entire Balkan peninsula (sometimes anachronistically called 'Moesia' by the ancient historians). Indeed, Gaius Poppaeus Sabinus, the governor from AD 11 until he died in

AD 35, had earned *ornamenta triumphalia* in AD 26 for crushing an uprising in western Thrace, where the tribes were being conscripted into auxiliary units. However, it was left to Claudius the organizer, in AD 44, to restore the region into three distinct provinces: Macedonia and Achaea were returned to the senate to be governed by proconsuls, while the northern area was formally constituted into the imperial consular province of Moesia. The first governor of Moesia was Aulus Didius Gallus, who received *ornamenta triumphalia* for action in the Bosporan kingdom, across the Black Sea in the Crimea, where he had installed a new 'friendly king'. Two years later, the kingdom of Thrace became the procuratorial province of Thracia.

In Britain, Plautius was replaced by Publius Ostorius Scapula; by AD 51, he had founded a *colonia* on the site of Camulodunum and had finally captured Caratacus. Scapula won *ornamenta triumphalia* and Claudius erected a triumphal arch at Rome, according to the inscription (only a fragment of which survives), 'because he received the surrender of 11 kings of the Britons, conquered without any loss' (*ILS* 216). The 11 tribes are not named, but the Iceni of present-day Norfolk and the Brigantes, whose lands stretched across the whole of northern England, must have pledged their allegiance to Rome. Unfortunately, hostilities continued in the west, and Scapula's death in office required the hasty despatch of Didius Gallus (who had perhaps held the prestigious proconsulship of Asia in the meantime).

The youthful tyrant

On Claudius' sudden (and suspicious) death in AD 54, his adopted son, the 16-year-old Nero, became emperor. One of his first acts was to shower the Praetorian Guard with a bonus of 15,000 sesterces per man (following one of Claudius' less worthy precedents). His first years as emperor were carefully supervised by his tutor, the philosopher

Seneca, and the Praetorian Prefect, Sextus Afranius Burrus. However, in AD 62, the former's retirement and the latter's death removed all restraint from the headstrong emperor; thereafter, his reign descended into tyranny, encouraged by the dark influence of Ofonius Tigellinus, the new Praetorian Prefect. Potential rivals were eliminated or, like Galba, sent to far-off governorships (in Galba's case, Tarraconensis), hopefully to be forgotten there.

Meanwhile, the conquest of Britain dragged on. Didius Gallus had been obliged to bolster the position of the 'friendly queen' of the Brigantes, Cartimandua, and perhaps installed Roman troops in her kingdom (as he had done in his earlier dealings with the Bosporan kingdom), but made little headway against the unruly Silures and Ordovices of what is now Wales. Gallus' successor in AD 57, Quintus Veranius, died within a year, boasting in his last testament that 'he would have subjugated the province if he had lived for another two years' (Tacitus, *Annals* 14.29.1).

The claim was hopelessly optimistic. His successor, Suetonius Paullinus, another man of proven military ability, overran the Welsh tribes in two campaigning seasons, before he was halted in his tracks by the so-called Boudican Revolt. The death of the 'friendly king' of the Iceni had prompted the annexation of his kingdom. However, this had been grossly mishandled, chiefly by Nero's rapacious financial procurator, and the tribe (led by the king's widow, Boudica) had risen in revolt; the neighbouring tribes joined them and inflicted serious damage on the province, including the sack of the *colonia* at Camulodunum. Although Paullinus eventually won a decisive victory (it was probably on this occasion that the Twentieth Legion took the titles 'Valeria Victrix', which it proudly bore thereafter), scaremongering by the financial procurator alarmed Nero, so that he allegedly considered abandoning the province altogether. When the true state of affairs became clear, Nero took an imperatorial acclamation for himself but conspicuously

bestowed no honours on Paullinus. In AD 61, a new governor was sent, Publius Petronius Turpilianus, who was probably a close relative of Aulus Plautius and deemed to be a 'safe pair of hands'; his three-year term was marked by inactivity.

Germany had remained quiet during these years, but the action of Lucius Duvius Avitus, commander on the lower Rhine, in expelling the Frisii in AD 57 from lands reserved for the army's use allowed Nero to take a third imperatorial acclamation. Typically, Avitus received no honours. And none were forthcoming either for his actions in the following year, when, in concert with his colleague on the upper Rhine, Titus Curtilius Mancia, he dispersed a coalition of tribes who were trying to occupy the same area of Roman lands. Nero, again, took an imperatorial acclamation.

Throughout Nero's reign, the eastern frontier, which had been quiet under Claudius, simmered and flared from crisis to crisis. At the outset, in AD 54, the Parthian King Vologaeses I had installed his brother, Tiridates, on the Armenian throne, in blatant contravention of the Augustan agreement. This was a serious threat to Roman prestige. Nero (or, more accurately, Nero's advisors) sent Corbulo – a veteran of the Rhine frontier who had meanwhile held the prestigious proconsulship of Asia – 'to secure Armenia' (the precise terms of his command, preserved by Tacitus, *Annals* 13.8). In order to provide him with the necessary resources, the provinces of Asia Minor were reorganized and Corbulo was appointed governor of an enlarged and amalgamated Cappadocia–Galatia.

Although Galatia was a fertile recruiting ground for the eastern legions, neither it nor its neighbour were armed provinces, so two of the four Syrian legions – the Third Gallica and the Sixth Ferrata – were ordered north, along with a detachment of the Tenth Fretensis, and placed under Corbulo's command. Simultaneously, the Fourth Scythica Legion began marching east to reinforce Syria; its place in Moesia was taken by the Seventh Claudia from Dalmatia.

The Roman world under the Julio-Claudian emperors, AD 14–68

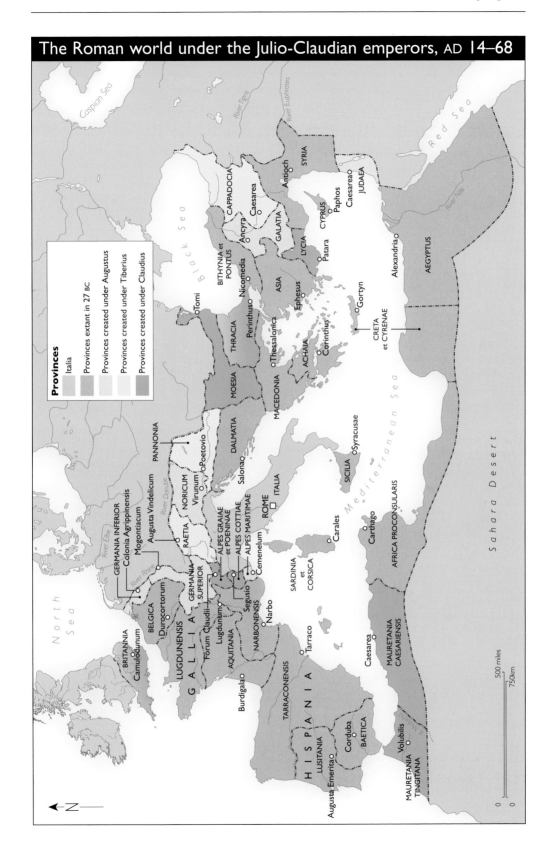

Provinces

- Italia
- Provinces extant in 27 BC
- Provinces created under Augustus
- Provinces created under Tiberius
- Provinces created under Claudius

Caspian Sea

Red Sea

River Tigris

River Euphrates

River Nile

SYRIA

Antioch

Caesarea

JUDAEA

CAPPADOCIA

Caesarea

GALATIA

CYPRUS

Paphos

Ancyra

LYCIA

Patara

Alexandria

AEGYPTUS

Black Sea

BITHYNIA et PONTUS

Nicomedia

ASIA

Ephesus

Tomi

THRACIA

Perinthus

Thessalonica

ACHAIA

Corinthus

Gortyn

CRETA et CYRENAE

Mediterranean Sea

MOESIA

MACEDONIA

DALMATIA

Salona

PANNONIA

Poetovio

Virunum

NORICUM

RAETIA

Augusta Vindelicum

Syracusae

SICILIA

ITALIA

ROME

Carales

Carthago

AFRICA PROCONSULARIS

Sahara Desert

GERMANIA INFERIOR

Colonia Agrippinensis

Mogontiacum

River Elbe

River Rhine

River Danube

ALPES GRAIAE et POENINAE

ALPES COTTIAE

ALPES MARITIMAE

Cemenelum

Segusio

GERMANIA SUPERIOR

GALLIA

Forum Claudii

Lugdunum

AQUITANIA

LUGDUNENSIS

BELGICA

Durocortorum

BRITANNIA

Camulodunum

North Sea

Narbo

NARBONENSIS

Burdigala

SARDINIA et CORSICA

Tarraco

TARRACONENSIS

HISPANIA

LUSITANIA

Augusta Emerita

Corduba

BAETICA

Caesarea

MAURETANIA CAESARIENSIS

Volubilis

MAURETANIA TINGITANA

500 miles

750km

←N—

Long years of inactivity had sapped the eastern legions, and Corbulo was obliged to impose his 'old school' discipline with field exercises and manoeuvres (Tacitus, *Annals* 13.35 recounts lurid details), while the routine administration of the province was handled by a subordinate legate, Gaius Rutilius Gallicus. Corbulo advised Vologaeses 'to choose peace over war and hand over hostages' (*Annals* 13.9); the king welcomed the delay, as trouble loomed on the Parthians' eastern frontier, so hostages were duly surrendered. But no promise of peace was forthcoming.

By AD 57 or 58, Corbulo was ready to move and invaded Armenia. As Tiridates was unwilling to meet him in battle, he was obliged to reduce his strongholds piecemeal, and finally captured the capital at Artaxata, whereupon the senate voted Nero extravagant honours – the emperor had already taken two or three imperatorial acclamations during this conflict – including a triumphal arch at Rome. However, the crisis had not yet been averted. It was only in AD 59 or 60, with Tiridates in flight and Nero's new nominee, Tigranes (a prince who traced his lineage back to Herod the Great), installed on the Armenian throne, that Corbulo could stand down.

At around the same time, the governor of Syria, the elderly Gaius Ummidius Quadratus, died, and Corbulo was instructed to fill this key vacancy. Realizing the fragility of the peace with Parthia – for the new king of Armenia had started throwing his weight around already, by raiding the lands of his pro-Parthian neighbours – Corbulo immediately placed the legions of Syria (now numbering five) on high alert and requested that Nero send a commander to defend Armenia. (Gallicus may still have been in the now-demilitarized Cappadocia–Galatia, but he lacked the seniority for a major military command.) Nero's choice fell upon Lucius Junius Caesennius Paetus (Turpilianus' colleague in the consulship for AD 61) to take over Cappadocia–Galatia. At the same time, the Fifth Macedonica Legion was ordered east from Moesia.

Meanwhile, however, Corbulo's fears had been realized. Even before his message reached Nero (for communication with the eastern frontier took several months), the Parthians had invaded Armenia with a view to reinstating Tiridates as king. Luckily, they were foiled by the defences of Tigranocerta, where Tigranes had taken refuge, so when Corbulo sent two legions (the Fourth Scythica and Twelfth Fulminata), Vologaeses was persuaded to withdraw, and decided instead to send a delegation to Nero. But Paetus arrived in his province with hopes of glory, so that, when the Parthian embassy returned empty-handed and Vologaeses renewed hostilities, the new governor eagerly launched a counter-strike with the two legions sent by Corbulo. Things went well at first and Nero proclaimed a great victory, but when Vologaeses' full army appeared at Rhandeia, Paetus lost his nerve and appealed to Corbulo for assistance. Scarcely had the message been sent than Paetus surrendered to the enemy, causing a general rout as Roman troops fled from Armenia.

Corbulo's Syrian garrison stood firm and the Parthians were persuaded to evacuate Armenia, on condition that Rome would respect the status quo, provided Tiridates agreed to receive his crown from Nero; Paetus was recalled (though he went unpunished for having caused the débâcle). When the second Parthian embassy arrived in Rome early in AD 63, it was clear that Vologaeses had reneged on the agreement, for there was no sign of Tiridates. Consequently, Nero had a choice to make: 'an unpredictable war or a shameful peace', as Tacitus put it (*Annals* 15.25). He chose to risk war and again placed his reliance upon Corbulo, who marched into Armenia with a massive army comprising his favourite legions, the Third Gallica and Sixth Ferrata, as well as the Fifth Macedonica, the Fifteenth Apollinaris (drafted in from Pannonia, where the vacancy was filled by the Tenth Gemina from Spain), and detachments from the two Egyptian legions. His aim was to restore Roman prestige by the appearance of overwhelming might. This time, Tiridates was eager to comply.

During the Armenian crisis, interesting events had been unfolding on the lower Danube. Nero's governor of Moesia, the same Plautius Silvanus who had accompanied the emperor Claudius to Britain, received 100,000 Transdanubian refugees, perhaps the first sign of the great movements of peoples across Europe. And, despite the fact that he had contributed a legion to Corbulo's war, he also acted in support of the Dacian kingdom in present-day Romania and the neighbouring tribes of the Roxolani and Bastarnae, who were beset by migrating Sarmatian tribes. He even (like Didius Gallus before him) intervened in the 'friendly kingdom' of the Crimea, and was allegedly 'the first to alleviate the grain supply of the Roman people by means of a large quantity of wheat from this province' (*ILS* 986).

Either as a result of this contact with Sarmatians, or because of the fragility of the Armenian solution, Nero planned an expedition 'to the Caspian Gates, for the war that he was preparing against the Albani' (Tacitus, *Histories* 1.6). The expedition, as Pliny pointed out, was really aimed at the Dariel Pass in Georgia ('which we can declare to be called the "Gates of the Caucasus", for maps sent from there have this name written on them'; Pliny, *Natural History* 6.40) and the tribe was the Alani, a Sarmatian people who would cause trouble for later emperors. A new legion, the First Italica, was raised with this expedition in mind, and the Fourteenth Gemina Legion was summoned from Britain. Simultaneously, Nero appears to have had designs on Ethiopia. In AD 61, he had sent a party of Praetorian explorers 900-odd miles up the Nile. Now, troops were en route to an assembly point at Alexandria, including the Fifteenth Apollinaris Legion, lately with Corbulo in Armenia.

In AD 66, a further round of celebrations ensued at Rome, greeting Tiridates' tardy visit. 'Hailed as imperator because of this, and laurels having been carried to the Capitol', wrote the biographer Suetonius, 'Nero closed the double doors of the Temple of Janus, just as if there were no wars' (*Life of Nero* 13.2). Similarly, his coinage

proclaimed to any who could read it that 'the peace of the Roman people has been imposed across the land and sea'. The torpor of Turpilianus' successor in Britain, Marcus Trebellius Maximus, made this technically true, but only briefly, for Nero's peace was about to be shattered.

In ostentatiously closing the Temple of Janus's doors, he was consciously emulating Augustus, and, like the first emperor, he adopted the title *imperator* as his first name. However, Nero was no Augustus. His increasing profligacy led to delays in army pay and the suspension of the grain dole to the populace at Rome, while the coinage began to be debased as a cost-cutting measure. Unrest followed. The uncovering of a conspiracy in AD 65 led to over a dozen high-profile executions and enforced suicides, and when the emperor travelled to Greece to pursue his musical ambitions, another conspiracy implicated Corbulo – or was made to appear so, as an excuse for the paranoid emperor to remove an imagined rival. The great general preferred to take his own life than wait for Nero to decide his fate.

By this point, the Jerusalem Jews were in revolt, having endured a succession of heavy-handed and rapacious procurators. To everyone's surprise, the governor of neighbouring Syria, Gaius Cestius Gallus, with all the military resources of that province, bungled his mission to reassert Roman order; beating a hasty retreat, the Twelfth Fulminata Legion suffered a humiliating defeat at the hands of Jewish guerrilla bands. Gallus' death soon after, from shame or old age, left vacancies in both Syria and Judaea. The first was filled by Gaius Licinius Mucianus, who had commanded one of Corbulo's legions in Armenia; the second was given to an older man of undistinguished career, who happened to be among Nero's retinue in Greece: Vespasian. Despite the procuratorial status of the province, the command of a task force comprising two Syrian legions – the Tenth Fretensis, commanded by Marcus Ulpius Traianus (father of the future emperor Trajan), and the Fifth Macedonica – and the

Herod the Great's impregnable palace-fortress at Masada was seized by bandits in AD 66, on the outbreak of the Jewish War. It was used as their base of operations until the arrival of the Tenth Fretensis Legion in the winter of AD 73/74, whereupon the entire plateau was ringed with Roman siegeworks (one of the camps can be seen, bottom right) and a siege embankment was constructed, ascending the mountain from the west (left of photo). (© Richard T. Nowitz/Corbis)

Fifteenth Apollinaris (placed under the command of Vespasian's son Titus) required consular authority, similar to that of the Rhine commanders; although Vespasian hadn't seen an army for 20 years, his consular status made him a suitable candidate. He was blessed with success, as two campaigning seasons served to secure the province and confine the insurgency to Jerusalem.

The governor of Lugdunensis, Gaius Julius Vindex, now raised the banner of revolt – according to Cassius Dio (*Roman History* 63.22.3), he accused Nero of having 'despoiled the entire Roman world' – and began to gather an army. Galba, who was still governor of Tarraconensis, watched from the sidelines and bided his time; supported only by the young governor of unarmed Lusitania, Marcus Salvius Otho, and with only a single legion (the Sixth Victrix) at his disposal, he began recruiting another (which he named the Seventh Galbiana). Meanwhile, Nero recalled the First Italica and Fourteenth Gemina legions, which were then in transit to the Caucasus, and began desperately raising troops at Rome; in Africa, it was perhaps on his behalf that the legate of the Third Augusta Legion, Lucius Clodius Macer, began recruiting a sister legion (apparently to be named the First Macriana Liberatrix, 'the liberator').

By June AD 68, the new commander of the upper Rhine legions, Lucius Verginius Rufus, had crushed Vindex's uprising at Vesontio, later declaring (on his tombstone, according to Pliny the Younger, *Letters* 6.10) that 'he claimed imperial power not for himself but for his fatherland' – proven, in fact, by his

The Levant at the time of Rome's First Jewish War, AD 66–74

N

Mediterranean Sea

GALILEE

Ptolemais○

Jotapata○   Taricheae○   *Sea of Galilee*

Tiberias○   ○Gamala

Mount Tabor▲   ○Gadara

Caesarea○   Scythopolis○

SAMARIA

River Jordan

Mount Gerizim▲

Joppa○

Beth-horon○

Jerusalem○

JUDAEA

Ascalon○   Herodium○

○Machaerus

Hebron○   *Dead Sea*

IDUMAEA   Masada○

0 ——— 25 miles
0 ——— 25km

refusal, not once but twice, to make himself emperor in Nero's place. However, the *praetoriani* had already selected a new emperor in Galba; once he was recognized by the senate, Nero committed suicide.

The Year of the Four Emperors (AD 69)

Galba was, by now, very old. He found Nero's treasury empty, so the donative of 30,000 sesterces expected by the *praetoriani* could not be paid. His parsimony was matched by his ingratitude: he passed over his loyal supporter Otho in his search for an heir. Likewise, when the commander on the lower Rhine, Fonteius Capito, was murdered by one of his legionary commanders, Fabius Valens, who claimed that he acted out of loyalty to Galba (perhaps hoping to be promoted in Capito's place), Galba installed Aulus Vitellius instead (allegedly on the grounds that such a glutton couldn't possibly present any threat). At the same time, the upright Verginius Rufus was quickly replaced by the ineffectual Titus Hordeonius Flaccus. Galba's arrogance and cruelty cannot have helped win supporters – for example, the elderly Turpilianus, whom Nero had put in charge of a task force to combat Vindex, was forced to commit suicide.

After only six months, Galba's reign was in trouble. The legions of the lower Rhine decided (perhaps encouraged by Valens) that they would prefer their own candidate to assume the purple: their commander, Vitellius. The army of the upper Rhine concurred. A fortnight later, Galba was dead, assassinated by the disgruntled *praetoriani*, and Otho had seized power. He hoped to curry favour with the army by rewarding the governors of Pannonia and Moesia with *ornamenta triumphalia* (the latter, Marcus Aponius Saturninus, had at least scored a success against the restless Transdanubian tribes), but Marcus Pompeius Silvanus, the legate of Dalmatia (with its single legion, the Eleventh Claudia), remained cautious,

and the armies on the Rhine (and in Britain) were beyond Otho's reach. Two task forces – based around the Fifth Alaudae Legion under Valens, and the Twenty-First Rapax under Caecina Alienus – had already set out to take Rome for Vitellius.

At Rome, Otho could count only on the Praetorians and the legion of marines that Nero had hastily enrolled (the future First Adiutrix Legion), so he had summoned the legions of Pannonia – the Thirteenth Gemina and Galba's Seventh Legion, which he had sent to Carnuntum to relieve the Tenth Gemina (now en route to Spain) – as well as the Fourteenth Gemina. He also called upon the legions of Moesia (the Seventh Claudia, Eighth Augusta and Third Gallica, newly transferred from the east). However, before they could arrive, Otho's forces had already been defeated near Cremona, and the emperor of three months committed suicide.

Vitellius dismissed Otho's legions and processed grandly into Italy. However, the eastern armies had not yet expressed their opinion, and, on 1 July, Vespasian was hailed as emperor by the Prefect of Egypt, Tiberius Julius Alexander, and his two legions (the Third Cyrenaica and Twenty-Second Deiotariana). The three legions in Judaea, followed by the three legions in Syria, quickly gave their support, and an army – based around the Sixth Ferrata Legion – set out for Europe. The Moesian legions joined them, and then those of Pannonia and Dalmatia. While Vespasian remained in the east, his generals met those of Vitellius, again near Cremona, and inflicted a crushing defeat. When the victorious army descended upon Rome, Vitellius was killed and the senate belatedly recognized Vespasian as their new emperor. An edict subsequently confirmed that (among other things) 'he shall have the right to make treaties with whomsoever he wishes, just like the deified Augustus and Tiberius Julius Caesar Augustus and Tiberius Claudius Caesar Augustus Germanicus' (*ILS* 244), appealing to the precedent set by his three 'good' predecessors.

In the Rhineland, the fighting continued into the following year. The tribe of the Batavi, under their leader Julius Civilis, had been encouraged to rise in support of Vespasian against the Vitellian legions. Events spiralled out of control, as the German Bructeri and the Gallic Treveri and Lingones joined the revolt. Vespasian's son-in-law, the fiery Quintus Petillius Cerialis, was sent north with a task force to pacify the lower Rhineland. By late summer, just as Titus's army (having captured Jerusalem and destroyed Herod's great Temple) were mopping up after the bloody Jewish Revolt, Cerialis could report that he had quelled the so-called Batavian Revolt. The Roman empire was once more at peace.

Stabilizing the state

Early in AD 69, the Sarmatian tribe of the Roxolani had invaded Moesia, but were defeated by the Third Gallica Legion (temporarily detached from the Syrian army for service on the lower Danube); the governor, Marcus Aponius Saturninus, was rewarded with *ornamenta triumphalia* (but was less successful, fortunately, in his subsequent attempt to murder one of his own legionary commanders, Lucius Tettius Julianus). The Dacians, too, seeing that the Roman world was in turmoil, had crossed the river, but were met by the Sixth Ferrata, en route to Italy in support of Vespasian's bid for the purple. Mucianus, the army commander, was rewarded with *ornamenta triumphalia*, Tacitus says, 'for his Sarmatian expedition' (*Histories* 4.4), so the Roxolani may still have been causing trouble. And in AD 70, the new Moesian governor himself, Gaius Fonteius Agrippa, fell in battle with Sarmatian tribes: 'they overran the entire area that was under his command, ravaging everything they encountered' (Josephus, *The Jewish War* 7.91). Moesia had clearly become a new flashpoint. Agrippa's successor, Rubrius Gallus, was obliged to strengthen his defences.

The Rhineland, too, required the new emperor's attention, as the Batavian Revolt had seen the mutiny of three legions (the First Germanica, the Fourth Macedonica and the Sixteenth Gallica), the mauling of a fourth (the Fifth Alaudae) and the destruction of a fifth (the Fifteenth Primigenia). Vespasian's answer was to strike them all from the army list and to muster two new legions, the Fourth Flavia and Sixteenth Flavia, in their place ('Flavia' recalling his family name). In the general reshuffling of the Rhine legions which ensued, the Fourth Flavia was swapped with the Eleventh Claudia, so that Dalmatia retained a legion, and the Sixteenth Flavia was sent east. The Seventh Galbiana Legion, destined to be the new garrison of Tarraconensis, was renamed 'Gemina' (a name that normally indicates some kind of amalgamation, perhaps, in this case, with elements of the disbanded legions). Meanwhile, Nero's First Italica was sent to Moesia, to allow the Eighth Augusta to transfer west; Nero's First Adiutrix was settled at Mainz; and a Second Adiutrix Legion was now raised and sent to Britain to fill the gap left by the Fourteenth Gemina

Gold *aureus* of the emperor Vespasian. He and his sons took the names Imperator Caesar Augustus (here abbreviated as IMP CAESAR AVG) as their own, consciously evoking a link with the emperor Augustus. (De Agostini/Getty Images)

(also stationed at Mainz). The total number of legions now stood at 28.

During Vespasian's reign, the commander on the upper Rhine, Gnaeus Pinarius Clemens, busied his legions clearing a way through the Black Forest, to create an important link between the upper Rhine and Danube; 'a road was driven from Strassbourg into Raetia', as one of the surviving milestones (*ILS* 5832) explains. For this (or for some related action about which we know nothing), he received *ornamenta triumphalia*. Affairs in Gaul and the Rhineland might, by now, have been put to rights after the Batavian Revolt, but Vespasian had not forgotten the role played by the Bructeri. Consequently, in about AD 76, the commander on the lower Rhine, Rutilius Gallicus (just one of several protégés of Corbulo to find favour with the new regime), invaded the tribe's territory and captured their formidable priestess Veleda.

In the east, Vespasian upgraded Judaea to the status of a praetorian province,

governed by the legate who commanded the Tenth Fretensis Legion. The first holders of this post, however, still had work to do, reducing the rebellious strongholds of Herodium, Machaerus and finally Masada, famously besieged by Lucius Flavius Silva in the early months of AD 74. There, the bandits known as *sicarii* ('knife-men') took their own lives, just as the Roman siege embankment reached their lofty haven; Silva received no *ornamenta triumphalia* for his victory, as the war had already been won by Titus,

but he was subsequently honoured with the ordinary consulship in AD 81.

In Syria, Mucianus handed the governorship over to Caesennius Paetus (the husband of Vespasian's niece, evidently forgiven for his shameful blunder under Corbulo), and, in AD 72, the tiny kingdom of Commagene was, once more, annexed to its larger neighbour. At the same time, the vast Cappadocia–Galatia agglomeration was retained as a watch on the long upper Euphrates border, chiefly, according to Suetonius, 'on account of the barbarians' unremitting incursions' (*Life of the Deified Vespasian* 8.4). It seems that the Caucasus had been affected by the same Sarmatian migrations that brought the Jazyges to the Pannonian border, but here the main culprits were the Alani. Roman troops were even outposted to the east, in the friendly Iberian kingdom (present-day Georgia), where they built a fort near modern-day Tbilisi. Cappadocia received two legions (the Twelfth Fulminata and, a little later, the Sixteenth Flavia), which entailed an upgrade to consular status (and the appointment of a separate praetorian *legatus* to assist the governor, as under Corbulo).

A few years later, when Traianus was governor of Syria, the Parthians requested Roman assistance against an incursion by the Alani, but were refused. It was perhaps in connection with these events that Traianus earned *ornamenta triumphalia* and patrician status for his family; he was also responsible for upgrading the Syrian road network, including driving a road east through Palmyra to the Euphrates, but this was hardly worthy of triumphal ornaments.

Only in Britain, where the process of repair after the damaging Boudican revolt continued, did Vespasian annex new

The 1849 painting *The Siege and Destruction of Jerusalem by the Romans under the command of Titus* depicts the Roman assault of AD 70 on the outer walls from Mount Scopus, to the north of the city. The Jewish Temple (centre left), protected by formidable defences, represented the focus of the insurgents' resistance. (Lithograph by Louis Haghe, after a lost original by David Roberts, Bridgeman via Getty)

Copy of the south panel from the Arch of Titus at Rome, depicting Roman soldiers carrying the spoils from the Jewish Temple in Jerusalem, during the triumphal procession in AD 71. The historian Josephus, describing the procession, makes particular mention of the golden table and seven-branched lampstand (the *menorah*). (Steerpike/CC-BY-3.0)

territory. Three capable legates, one after the other – Petillius Cerialis, Sextus Julius Frontinus and Gnaeus Julius Agricola – drove Roman arms forward, until Agricola (a previous legionary commander in Britain) penetrated present-day Scotland.

In essence, Vespasian's reign harked back to the Augustan peace. He emulated the first emperor by adopting the names Imperator Caesar Augustus (as did his successors), and, just as Augustus had done, he made his mark on the Roman populace by staging a grand triumph, jointly with his son Titus in summer AD 71, to celebrate 'Judaea captured', as the coins proclaimed; the crowd would not see another for over 40 years. The doors of the Temple of Janus were once more closed (although, strictly speaking, war continued in Britain), and work commenced on an enormous Temple of Pax (the goddess of peace), which would be the repository of the treasures from Jerusalem; the loot from the war paid for the building of the great Flavian amphitheatre (nowadays known as the Colosseum).

Conqueror of Jerusalem

From the beginning of Vespasian's reign, his 30-year-old son Titus was associated with him as junior colleague. The biographer Suetonius called him 'partner and protector in empire' (*Life of the Deified Titus* 5.2) – 'protector' because, unusually, he occupied the post of *praefectus praetorio*, normally the prerogative of an equestrian, and commanded a reorganized Praetorian Guard; and 'partner' because the pair frequently took the ordinary consulship and, from AD 71, Titus was granted the annually renewed *tribunicia potestas* (in some ways, the key to imperial power). Likewise, whenever Vespasian took an imperatorial acclamation, so did Titus (though always remaining six behind his father's total). Meanwhile, his teenaged brother Domitian received fewer honours, though in AD 73 he held the ordinary consulship at the age of 21, at least 11 years earlier than Augustus' rules allowed.

It was natural that, when Vespasian died in June AD 79, Titus (now in his 40th year) became emperor. His short reign was marred by the twin disasters of the eruption of Vesuvius (in which his friend Pliny, the encyclopaedist, died) and a great fire at Rome, but he still enjoyed popular fame as the conqueror of Jerusalem. The opening of the Colosseum in AD 80 was celebrated with an unprecedented 100 days of spectacular public shows – it may have been on this occasion that the poet Martial saw a condemned criminal 'surrender his naked organs to a Caledonian bear' (*On Spectacles* 7) – and the erection of two triumphal arches (only one of which still stands) continued to provide work for Roman labourers right up to the emperor's death in September AD 81. (The surviving arch is dedicated posthumously to Titus, but medieval records of the other arch show that it carried a long inscription, making the exaggerated claim that 'at his father's command and with his advice and guidance, he subdued the Jewish people and destroyed the city of Jerusalem, which had either been attacked in vain by generals, kings or peoples before him, or hadn't even been attempted'; *ILS* 264.)

The Arch of Titus in the Roman Forum (here viewed from below) was completed in AD 81, shortly after that emperor's death. It commemorates his famous victory over the Jews, which culminated in the destruction of Jerusalem. The two main decorative panels depict scenes from the triumphal procession of Vespasian and Titus ten years earlier. (Sebastian Bergmann/CC-BY-SA-2.0)

In Britain, it is possible that Titus ordered Agricola to consolidate his gains at the Forth–Clyde isthmus, which, according to Tacitus, 'was now secured by garrisons and the whole interior on the nearer side was being mastered, the enemy having been pushed back as if into a different island' (*Life of Agricola* 23). Certainly, the historian Cassius Dio links the emperor's fifteenth imperatorial acclamation (datable to the final months of AD 79) to events in Britain. Nowhere else had Augustus' empire been significantly extended.

The frontiers under pressure

On Titus's death, the *praetoriani* acclaimed his brother, now almost 30 years old, *imperator* in his place. Unfortunately, Domitian had not been prepared for the task. Nevertheless, he began enthusiastically, and set about garnering the military glory that he, like Claudius on his accession, conspicuously lacked. His second imperatorial acclamation was taken in AD 82, possibly for successes in Britain, reversing (or capitalizing on) his brother's policy of

consolidation. Thereafter, they followed in a steady stream, until, over the course of a 15-year reign, he surpassed his father's 20 acclamations. In addition, besides virtually monopolizing the ordinary consulship for years on end, he staged at least two grand triumphal processions at Rome, as befitted the first reigning emperor since Augustus to accompany the legions on campaign.

Early in AD 83, casting around for a military adventure of his own, he rushed north to Germany, where he perhaps relieved Quintus Corellius Rufus of his command over the army of the upper Rhine, for he was not a well man (though Pliny the Younger, *Letters* 1.12.8, quotes him as saying that he struggled on through illness 'so that I can outlive that bandit' – referring to Domitian – 'by even a single day!'). Domitian's expedition was directed at the Chatti, who (according to Frontinus) were spoiling for a fight. Conscription among the

Reconstructed gateway of the Roman fort of Vetoniana (present-day Pfünz, in Bavaria), on the Danube frontier of Raetia. Originally built under the emperor Domitian, it was probably badly damaged during the Marcomannic Wars, requiring substantial refurbishment in the AD 180s. (Andreas Strauss/Getty)

German tribes (like the Usipi, who mutinied when sent to serve in the garrison of Britain) had perhaps stirred up old animosities, but the Chatti had never been friends of Rome. 'Domitian safeguarded Roman territory', writes Frontinus (*Stratagems* 1.1.8), 'by launching a surprise attack and breaking the fierce spirit of this savage nation'.

Domitian took the war seriously. It was probably at this time that a new legion, the First Minervia, was enrolled and sent to Bonna (modern-day Bonn) to release the Twenty-First Rapax for service against the Chatti. Reinforcements came from as far afield as Britain, from where Lucius Roscius Aelianus, 'military tribune of the Ninth Hispana Legion, commanded detachments of that legion on the German expedition' (*ILS* 1025). By late summer, Domitian had been acclaimed *imperator* again (probably twice) and was able to add *Germanicus* ('conqueror of the Germans') to his official titles, styling himself thereafter as Imperator Caesar Domitian Augustus Germanicus. The war apparently continued, for it was not until AD 85 that Domitian's coinage proclaimed 'Germany captured'.

Meanwhile, in north Africa, the desert tribe of the Nasamones had rebelled against

Modern rock-cut sculpture representing King Decebalus, overlooking the Kazan or 'Iron Gates' gorge of the River Danube, just upriver from the site of Apollodorus' famous bridge.

Roman taxation and were ruthlessly annihilated by the Third Augusta Legion. Domitian's pompous pronouncement, that 'I have forbidden the Nasamones to exist' (Cassius Dio, *Roman History* 67.5.6), cannot have endeared him to a senate that already balked at addressing him as 'lord and god'. Trouble in Mauretania was crushed, as well.

In Britain, the Caledonian tribes had likewise been crushed, but Agricola's victory in battle at Mons Graupius was not broadcast in German fashion, owing to the emperor's lack of involvement. Nevertheless, Domitian surely took an imperatorial acclamation (one of the three taken during AD 84, by the time news of the victory reached Rome) and Agricola himself was rewarded with *ornamenta triumphalia* (a rare honour from an emperor more used to distributing the lesser *dona militaria*, 'military decorations'). However, the general's son-in-law, Tacitus, expected grander treatment for the conqueror of

Caledonia, and his commentary on Domitian's reign is, in consequence, snide and bitter: he complained that 'Britain was conquered and immediately let go' (*Histories* 1.2.1). But it was natural that the inexperienced emperor should celebrate his own successes in grander style than the successes of his subordinates.

Moreover, Domitian's attention was directed elsewhere, for a storm was slowly gathering on the Danube. An auxiliary diploma from Moesia reveals that, even during the Chattan War, three units had been drafted in from the army of the upper Rhine. Others were to follow. The *consilium* ('council') summoned to convene at the emperor's villa – the satirist Juvenal mischievously suggests that they were there to discuss how best to divide up a large and delicious turbot – included knowledgeable military men, whom Juvenal acknowledges were really 'planning battles in the marble villa' (*Satires* 4.112). Among them were Rubrius Gallus, 'Pegasus' (a previous governor of Dalmatia, thought to be the brother of 'Griffin', Decimus Plotius Grypus), Rutilius Gallicus, and the emperor's *praefectus praetorio* Cornelius Fuscus, a man (according to Tacitus,

Histories 2.86) whose 'desire for neutrality led him to renounce his senatorial status'.

In AD 85, the Dacians made their move under their king Decebalus, crossing the frozen Danube and plundering Moesia. The Roman governor, Oppius Sabinus, was killed in battle, and the commander of the Seventh Claudia Legion stepped into the breach until a new consular governor (Marcus Cornelius Nigrinus) could be appointed. It may be that the Dacians had surprised Sabinus by sweeping across the Dobrudja region of the lower Danube, and that the so-called mausoleum at Adamklissi (near the later Tropaeum Traiani) marks the scene of the defeat. Domitian rushed to the war zone and, in a highly unorthodox move, gave overall command to the equestrian Fuscus. A further two or three imperatorial acclamations followed, and the wily Decebalus sued for peace. Domitian returned to Rome, and in the following year, 'after various battles, he staged a double triumph over the Chatti and the Dacians' (Suetonius, *Life of Domitian* 6.1), distributing largesse to the city populace and increasing the army's pay (the first increase since the days of Augustus).

Domitian was under no illusions that the Danube was now at peace. Legions were mobilized to augment the Pannonian and Moesian garrisons: the First Adiutrix moved from the Rhine and the Second Adiutrix was withdrawn from Britain, occasioning retrenchment and the abandonment of the fortress at Inchtuthil (near Perth in Scotland) before it was even completed. Furthermore, Moesia was divided into two provinces, in order to bring two consular governors to the troubled sector: Nigrinus retained Moesia Inferior, with the First Italica and Fifth Macedonica legions, while the venerable governor of Pannonia, Lucius Funisulanus Vettonianus, was moved to Moesia Superior, where the Seventh Claudia Legion was joined by the Fourth Flavia Legion (transferred from Dalmatia and causing that province to lose its consular status).

There must have been initial successes to justify Domitian's thirteenth and fourteenth imperatorial acclamations (and Nigrinus was

twice decorated with *dona militaria*), but in AD 87, a barren year for honours, disaster struck again: Fuscus was cut down on Dacian soil, where (in Juvenal's gruesome phrase) 'he delivered his entrails to the Dacian vultures' (*Satires* 4.111), and a Roman battle-standard was lost. The emperor himself again travelled to the war zone, where Vettonianus was replaced by a younger man, Tettius Julianus (another Flavian stalwart, whose equestrian brother – Vettonianus' son-in-law, in fact – had risen to the *praefectura Aegypti* under Titus). Penetrating Dacia's Carpathian fastness by way of the Iron Gate Pass, Julianus brought the Dacians to battle at Tapae and crushed them 'in great numbers' (Cassius Dio, *Roman History* 67.10.1–2, where he claims that Julianus ordered his men to paint their centurions' names on their shields, so that the bravest men could be identified and

A Roman legionary, armed with the characteristic rectangular body-shield (the so-called *scutum*) and the short cut-and-thrust sword (the *gladius*), attacks a Dacian warrior, armed with the characteristic two-handed *falx*. A Germanic barbarian, identifiable by his 'Suebian knot' hairstyle, has fallen injured at his feet, on one of the metopes from the Tropaeum Traiani. (CristianChirita/CC-BY-SA-3.0)

rewarded). Domitian felt able to take no fewer than six imperatorial acclamations during AD 88. However, events on the Rhine suddenly took the shine from Domitian's Dacian success.

In January AD 89, the commander of the upper army, Lucius Antonius Saturninus, raised the banner of revolt, having appropriated the pay chest of the two legions at Mainz, and might have succeeded in repeating Vitellius' success (exactly 20 years earlier), except that his Chattan allies were prevented from crossing the Rhine to join him by an unseasonal thaw. His lower Rhine counterpart, Aulus Lappius Maximus, chose to oppose him (and attempted to limit the damage done by the abortive coup by burning Saturninus' correspondence). Although the army of the lower Rhine was rewarded with the titles *pia fidelis Domitiana* ('loyal and faithful to Domitian') and Domitian perhaps chose the occasion to take a fresh acclamation (his twenty-first), Maximus himself received nothing from the ungrateful emperor besides an acknowledgement that he was *confector belli Germanici* ('the man who ended the German war', carefully avoiding mention of a revolt; *ILS* 1006) and a transfer to the governorship of Syria. The twin military commands on the Rhine were finally recognized as the consular provinces of Germania Inferior and Germania Superior, and the garrison of each was soon reduced to three legions. Saturninus's head was sent to Rome and his vacancy was filled by Lucius Javolenus Priscus.

Matters had been serious enough to merit the mobilization of the Seventh Gemina Legion, stationed in far-off Tarraconensis, inadvertently bringing its 35-year-old commander, Marcus Ulpius Trajanus, to centre stage (his reward, surely intended to round off a curiously lacklustre career, was the ordinary consulship for AD 91). The suspicious emperor decided henceforth to limit the funds stored in each legionary pay chest, and decreed that two legions should never again share a fortress (the legions of Egypt seem to have continued doing so,

but they were less of a threat, being under the command of the equestrian *praefectus Aegypti*). The circle of those chosen for punishment extended beyond the Rhineland. The governor of Britain, Lucius Sallustius Lucullus, perhaps now fell victim to the emperor's witch-hunt: Suetonius records that his alleged crime was 'having allowed spears of a new shape to be called Lucullean' (*Life of Domitian* 10.3), but his fatal mistake might have been to promise Saturninus the support of the British garrison.

Domitian now had breathing room to reflect on the lack of support that his supposed Suebian allies had provided during the recent Dacian War. This is the reason given by Cassius Dio for his immediate transit to Pannonia – probably in company with the Twenty-First Rapax Legion, banished from Mainz – but there may have been rumours of unrest among the Marcomanni and Quadi. In any event, he suffered a defeat and was fortunate that the Dacians were in no position to take advantage of Roman weakness. A generous peace was granted to Decebalus, along with 'large and immediate subsidies, and workmen skilled in all sorts of trades, both peaceful and warlike' (Cassius Dio, *Roman History* 67.7.4), and the emperor returned to Rome to celebrate another triumph with magnificent games and the erection of a massive equestrian statue.

However, even if the Suebians remained quiet, the Sarmatian problem had not been solved, and, early in AD 92, the Jazyges swept across the Pannonian border. Domitian launched an *expeditio Suebica et Sarmatica* ('expedition against the Suebians and Sarmatians'; *ILS* 1017), 'which was unavoidable', writes Suetonius (*Life of Domitian* 6.1), 'because a legion [no doubt the Twenty-First Rapax] had been destroyed with its commander'. Domitian's retribution was swift (he was back in Rome by January AD 93, having taken his twenty-second and last acclamation) and among the recipients of *dona militaria* was the commander of the Thirteenth Gemina Legion, Lucius

Ruins of the stronghold at Capalna in north-west Dacia. The inhospitable terrain and the formidable defences made the Dacian strongholds impregnable to any attacker without siege equipment. (România de vis/ CC-BY-SA-3.0-RO)

Caesennius Sospes (a son of Caesennius Paetus – his name means 'safe and sound', perhaps in reference to his survival of his father's Armenian disaster).

Like his father and brother, Domitian looked after Rome's populace with building projects and entertainment, but his increasingly tyrannical behaviour – perhaps understandable in a young man who was not only the son of a god, but the brother of one, too (for both Vespasian and Titus had been posthumously deified) – led to a palace coup in September AD 96, directed by his wife, Corbulo's daughter Domitia, and the *praefectus praetorio* Titus Petronius Secundus. In the aftermath, his successors had no reason to laud the dead emperor and every reason to blacken his name. He was likened to Nero, and the senate voted to officially erase all traces of him in a process known as *damnatio memoriae* ('condemnation of remembrance'). As far as inscriptional evidence is concerned, they were remarkably successful.

The murdered Domitian had no surviving relatives (most had fallen victim to the emperor's growing paranoia), so the senate elected as his replacement the venerable Marcus Cocceius Nerva, a three-times consul (a rare honour) who traced his lineage back to the days of Julius Caesar, a Galba to Domitian's Nero. However, facing growing discontent at Rome (for Domitian's assassination had evidently encouraged the governor of three-legion Syria, Cornelius Nigrinus, to contemplate emulating Vespasian's response to Nero's murder), Nerva reluctantly bolstered his position by manufacturing a rival *vir militaris* ('military man') to become his heir.

His choice fell upon Marcus Ulpius Trajanus (known to posterity as Trajan), a patrician whose career had languished under Domitian, but whom Nerva now plucked from the shadows – illustrating the power of patronage at Rome – and sent to govern Germania Superior. This was no random choice, for that province's three legions stood closest to Italy, and this time (unlike the situation in AD 89) their commander could count on the additional four legions of Germania Inferior (currently under Trajan's fellow Spaniard,

Lucius Licinius Sura). With Trajan's formal adoption in October AD 97, a clear message had been sent to Nigrinus (who was surely now silently removed, for the young commander of the Fourth Scythica Legion can be seen to have briefly stepped into the governor's shoes). Many must have travelled to Mainz to pay their respects to the new heir to the throne; among them was Trajan's young ward (the son of his deceased cousin) Publius Aelius Hadrianus (the future emperor Hadrian), then serving his tribunate in the Twenty-Second Primigenia Legion.

Nerva continued to rule throughout AD 97, but he was a puppet in the hands of the Trajanic faction, led (it would seem) by the *éminence grise* Frontinus, whom Tacitus rightly calls *vir magnus* ('a great man'). Frontinus was now rewarded with consulships in that year and in AD 100, when he and Trajan both held their third consulships together. Nerva's childlessness inaugurated a new phase of the Principate

When the emperor Domitian died in AD 96, the senate decreed an official sanction on his memory (*damnatio memoriae*). His statues were pulled down and his inscriptions defaced. (DEA/A. Dagli Orti/Getty)

in which successors happened to be selected (like Trajan), rather than foisted upon the empire (like Domitian).

Amid the machinations at Rome, the business of safeguarding the empire continued. Sura's predecessor in Germania Inferior, the aged Titus Vestricius Spurinna (a veteran of the 'Year of the Four Emperors'), had recently won *ornamenta triumphalia* (unthinkable under Domitian's regime) for 'blood, sweat and deeds' (in the words of Pliny, *Letters* 2.7.1). He had imposed a new king on the Bructeri, presumably after their pitiless massacre, 'not by Roman weapons and missiles, but, even more magnificent and a delight for the eyes', by their Germanic neighbours (Tacitus, *On Germany* 33).

Similarly, on the very eve of Trajan's adoption, 'laurels had been brought from Pannonia' (Pliny, *Panegyric on Trajan* 8.2), where Domitian's governor of Moesia Superior, Gnaeus Pompeius Longinus, had taken command; it was Roman practice to decorate victorious despatches with a laurel branch. Although the Sarmatian Jazyges were, for the moment, quiet, their Suebian neighbours, the Marcomanni and Quadi, had been causing trouble once again. Nerva and his new heir both took the title *Germanicus* ('conqueror of the Germans'), and *dona militaria* were distributed to the deserving officers, one set going to Quintus Attius Priscus, equestrian tribune of the First Adiutrix Legion (*ILS* 2720). Nerva perhaps hoped to foster loyalty among the four Pannonian legions (for the First and Second Adiutrix legions and the Thirteenth Gemina Legion had recently been reinforced by the Fourteenth Gemina, transferred from the Rhine probably to replace the lost Twenty-First Rapax).

However, the empire was about to see its first major expansion since Claudius' invasion of Britain, over half a century before.

War and conquest

When Nerva died in January AD 98, aged 67, Trajan was already emperor. However, it was fully a year before he left the frontier to visit Rome. As heir apparent, he had handed the governorship of Germania Superior over to Lucius Julius Servianus (Hadrian's brother-in-law), and perhaps now took the opportunity to visit the Danube frontier to view the Dacians for himself, as he was said to be 'troubled by the large subsidy they were receiving every year, having seen that their power and arrogance were on the increase' (Cassius Dio, *Roman History* 68.6.1). It may even have been at this point that the *equites singulares Augusti* ('the emperor's horse guard') were created, so that Trajan did not have to rely so heavily upon the fickle *praetoriani*.

Having returned to Rome for a year, Trajan set off for Dacia with a *consilium* that included the 25-year-old Hadrian, as well as Sura and Servianus. The three Danubian provinces by now mustered ten legions in total, mostly stationed on the right bank of the river. Not all could be released for an invasion of Dacia, so others were drafted in: the First Minervia and Tenth Gemina legions marched from Germania Inferior, and the Eleventh Claudia came from Germania Superior, under its commander Gaius Julius Quadratus Bassus.

Gold *aureus* of the emperor Trajan, showing the new title *Optimus* ('Best', here abbreviated as OPTIM) alongside his other titles *Germanicus* ('conqueror of the Germans', commemorating the victory of AD 97 over the Suebian tribes) and *Dacicus* ('conqueror of the Dacians', commemorating Trajan's first Dacian victory of AD 102). (De Agostini/Getty Images)

During the first campaigning season of this First Dacian War, the Dacian king Decebalus was defeated at Tapae (scene of Tettius Julianus' victory in AD 88) but refused to meet Trajan's envoys, Sura and Claudius Livianus (the *praefectus praetorio*). Meanwhile, engineering work was completed on a canal, perhaps begun by Domitian to bypass the Danube rapids as they flowed through the Iron Gates gorge, upstream from the fort at Drobeta, and a permanent bridge was constructed at the fort by the military engineer Apollodorus of Damascus, in order to make it easier to cross the river into Dacia.

Campaigning continued into the following year. An autonomous force of Moorish light horsemen under their chieftain, Lusius Quietus, scored notable successes, and it seems likely that Apollodorus' engineering talents were further employed in devising ways to capture the Dacian fortresses, for 'Trajan seized mountain strongholds, where he found arms and captured machinery and the battle-standard that had been taken from Fuscus' (Cassius Dio, *Roman History* 68.9.3). His ultimate goal was the Dacian capital at Sarmizegethusa Regia, which might well have proven impregnable, but for the fact that the governor of Moesia Inferior, Manlius Laberius Maximus, managed to capture some important prisoners, including Decebalus' family, thus persuading the Dacian king to agree to terms: namely, 'to hand over arms, machines and engineers, give up deserters, dismantle his fortifications, evacuate captured territory, acknowledge the same enemies and friends as the Romans, and neither shelter deserters nor entice soldiers from the Roman empire' (*ibid.* 68.9.5–6).

Trajan returned to Rome to celebrate a triumph as *Dacicus* ('conqueror of the Dacians'), and to share the ordinary consulship for AD 103 (his fifth) with Laberius Maximus, the captor of Decebalus' family. He had, in the meantime, acquired three imperatorial acclamations, making him IMP IV. The tally would not increase for another two years, but during the intervening calm, Decebalus was silently restocking his armoury and repairing his strongholds. Soon, it must have become clear that there could be no 'friendly kingdom' in Dacia, for Trajan had begun enrolling two new legions (the Second Traiana and Thirtieth Ulpia), a sure sign that annexation was in prospect.

By June AD 105, the senate had declared Decebalus an enemy once more, and Trajan (taking Hadrian with him in the role of legionary commander) was en route for Moesia. Seeing that Trajan meant business this time, Decebalus ('by guile and deceit', says Cassius Dio, *Roman History* 68.11.3) attempted to kill him by employing Roman deserters as assassins. The ploy failed, but the tale (preserved in the Augustan History's *Life of Hadrian* 4.8) that Trajan 'had once said to Lucius Neratius Priscus, "if misfortune befalls me, I entrust the provinces to you"', perhaps refers to this moment, when Priscus, as governor of Pannonia, would have been well placed to prosecute the war in Trajan's absence.

Cast of scene CXLV on Trajan's Column, showing Roman auxiliary cavalry attempting to capture the Dacian king Decebalus, who holds a curved dagger to his throat. The cavalryman stretching out to the king is evidently Tiberius Claudius Maximus, whose involvement is recorded on his tombstone. (Halibutt/CC-BY-3.0)

The remainder of the year was probably spent in communication with Decebalus, for he had invited Pompeius Longinus (a senior consular with knowledge of the area) to a parley, where he had treacherously taken him hostage to use as leverage in negotiations with Trajan. Longinus eventually resolved the stalemate by nobly committing suicide.

The Roman attack began in earnest in the following year, when a huge army crossed over Apollodorus' bridge. The details are lost to us, but the general course of both wars is clear from the massive bas-relief sculpture that spirals up Trajan's Column at Rome. We also catch glimpses from honorific inscriptions, such as the epitaph of Quadratus Bassus, 'appointed army commander in the [Second] Dacian War and a companion of the emperor Trajan in the war there, and honoured with triumphal ornaments' (*AE* 1933, 268).

Cassius Dio relates that 'as Decebalus's capital and country had been placed under complete occupation, and as he himself was at risk of capture, he took his own life, and his head was taken to Rome' (*Roman History* 68.14.3). The tombstone of the cavalryman

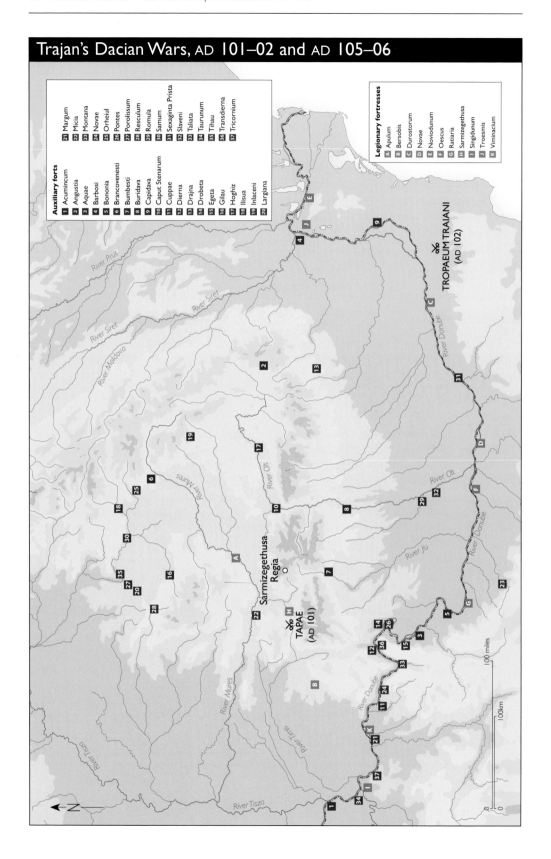

Trajan's Dacian Wars, AD 101–02 and AD 105–06

Auxiliary forts

1 Acumincum
2 Angustia
3 Aquae
4 Barbosi
5 Bononia
6 Brancovenesti
7 Bumbesti
8 Buridava
9 Capidava
10 Caput Stenarum
11 Cuppae
12 Dierna
13 Drajna
14 Drobeta
15 Egeta
16 Gilau
17 Hoghiz
18 Ilisua
19 Inlaceni
20 Largiana
21 Margum
22 Micia
23 Montana
24 Novae
25 Orheiul
26 Pontes
27 Porolissum
28 Resculum
29 Romula
30 Samum
31 Sexaginta Prista
32 Slaveni
33 Taliata
34 Taurunum
35 Tihau
36 Transdierna
37 Tricornium

Legionary fortresses

A Apulum
B Bersobis
C Durostorum
D Novae
E Noviodunum
F Oescus
G Ratiaria
H Sarmizegethusa
I Singidunum
J Troesmis
K Viminacium

TROPAEUM TRAIANI (AD 102)

Sarmizegethusa Regia

TAPAE (AD 101)

River Prut
River Siret
River Siret
River Moldova
River Mures
River Olt
River Mures
River Olt
River Jiu
River Danube
River Danube
River Danube
River Tisza
River Tisza
River Timis
River Tisza

100 miles
100 km

Rome's northern frontier in the 2nd century

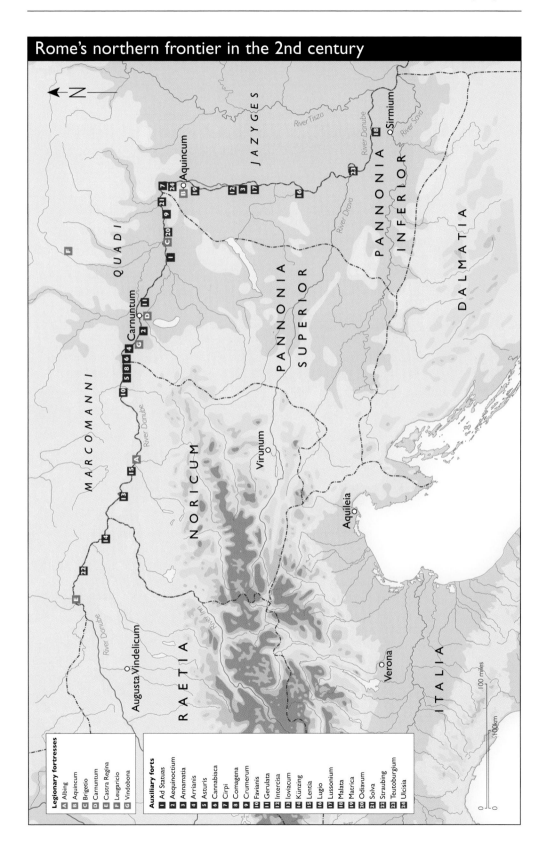

Legionary fortresses
- A Albing
- B Aquincum
- C Brigetio
- D Carnuntum
- E Castra Regina
- F Leugaricio
- G Vindobona

Auxiliary forts
- 1 Ad Statuas
- 2 Aequinoctium
- 3 Annamatia
- 4 Arrianis
- 5 Asturis
- 6 Cannabiaca
- 7 Cirpi
- 8 Comagena
- 9 Crumerum
- 10 Favianis
- 11 Gerulata
- 12 Intercisa
- 13 Ioviacum
- 14 Kunzing
- 15 Lentia
- 16 Lugio
- 17 Lussonium
- 18 Malata
- 19 Matrica
- 20 Odiavum
- 21 Solva
- 22 Straubing
- 23 Teutoburgium
- 24 Ulcisia

Tiberius Claudius Maximus (only discovered in 1965) sheds some interesting light on the story; erected many years later, after the emperor's death (and inevitable deification), it records how Maximus

was promoted to double-pay grade in the Second Squadron of Pannonians by the deified Trajan and assigned by him as a scout during the Dacian War, and was twice decorated for valour in the Dacian War … and was promoted to decurion ['troop-commander'] in the same squadron, because he hunted Decebalus down and carried his head to Trajan at Ranisstorum.

(AE 1969/70, 583; the placename is unknown)

Trajan set about organizing the kingdom as a two-legion province, and Pannonia was now divided into Pannonia Superior and Pannonia Inferior, to enable the governor of the latter (Hadrian, in fact) to keep a close watch on the Jazyges. Elsewhere, men were decorated and promoted, and units were rewarded for meritorious service. It was not until summer AD 107 that the emperor returned to Rome to stage his second triumph; by then, his friend and confidant Sura had already opened the year as ordinary consul (his third consulship, a rare honour). Public celebrations lasted 123 days, during which 10,000 gladiators performed and 11,000 animals were reportedly killed for entertainment. By the following year, the huge, cylindrical cenotaph known as the Tropaeum Traiani – ringed with sculptures, and visible from far and wide at over 100ft tall – had been erected at Adamklissi in Moesia Inferior (near the Roman mausoleum thought to mark the site of Oppius Sabinus' disaster 23 years earlier), broadcasting the message, through its dedication to Mars Ultor ('the Avenger'), that Roman defeats at the hands of the Dacians had been avenged.

Meanwhile, the new province of Arabia (spanning parts of modern Jordan and Saudi Arabia) had quietly been added to the empire, presumably on the death of the 'friendly king' there, by the governor of Syria,

Aulus Cornelius Palma (for which he seems to have gained *ornamenta triumphalia*; he certainly won a second consulship). A single legion (the Third Cyrenaica from Egypt) plus a handful of auxiliary units were installed as the garrison. Although the milestones along the *via nova Traiana* ('Trajan's new highway', running south from Syria to the Red Sea) proclaimed that Arabia had been 'reduced to the form of a province' (*ILS* 5834), there was a five-year delay before they were set up, and the slogan 'Arabia acquired' – an odd turn of phrase, rather than the expected 'captured' – only appeared on the coinage from AD 112. The intention was perhaps to avoid overshadowing the Dacian victory.

Building work continued apace at Rome, where an enormous new forum complex was under construction, re-using and re-interpreting Domitianic schemes and transforming the centre of the city. Trajan had already upgraded the Circus Maximus as 'a place that befits a people who are conquerors of nations' (Pliny, *Panegyric on Trajan* 51.3); the honorific inscription was apparently seen by Cassius Dio, who deplored its modesty in referring only to 'the addition of places' in the Circus, rather than a wholesale face-lift, 'through the generosity of the best of emperors' (*ILS* 286). However, from around this time, Trajan began to use the title *optimus princeps* ('the best emperor'), recalling (with breathtaking arrogance) the epithet of the supreme Roman god Jupiter, who was *optimus maximus* ('best and greatest').

Trajan's new forum was formally opened in AD 112, and its colossal centrepiece, nowadays known as Trajan's Column, was unveiled in May AD 113. The dedicatory inscription (*ILS* 294) shows that the emperor, who had already added two new provinces to the empire and had crushed the Dacians, was still only IMP VI, in stark contrast to Domitian's unseemly accumulation of acclamations. But his thirst for conquest had not yet been quenched.

A new opportunity for adventure now presented itself in the east, where the new Parthian king, Chosroes (having temporarily ousted Vologaeses III), had removed the

The inscription nowadays known as the *Tabula Traiana* (*AE* 1973, 475) records that, in AD 101, Trajan 'made the navigation of the Danube safe by diverting the river, on account of the dangerous rapids'. Work on the 3-mile canal bypassing the worst of the Iron Gates gorge had perhaps been begun under Domitian. (Rlichtefeld/ CC-BY-3.0)

Armenian king, Parthamasiris, and installed his own nominee. This was a clear violation of the Augustan settlement, which had been so thoroughly underlined by the achievements of Corbulo, 50 years before. The historian Cassius Dio relates how the Parthians, when they saw that Trajan was mobilizing for war, rushed to reinstate Parthamasiris, but their apology came too late. By AD 114, a large army had assembled in Cappadocia–Galatia, comprising all or parts of the seven eastern legions, reinforced by detachments from the Danubian legions; Lusius Quietus and his Moorish horsemen were included, once again. Trajan advanced into Armenia and arrangements were made to receive Parthamasiris at Elegeia, where the Armenian king expected to receive his diadem from the emperor, 'just as Tiridates had received it from Nero' (Cassius Dio,

Roman History 68.20.2). However, Trajan had other ideas, and declared Armenia a Roman province, though he pointedly refrained from taking an imperatorial acclamation, despite the fact that the reorganization appears to have involved some fighting.

Trajan now decided to press on into Mesopotamia, and battles clearly ensued in AD 115 (although we lack the details), for the emperor now took four imperatorial acclamations in quick succession. Edessa and Nisibis were captured, and by the following spring the emperor had entered Ctesiphon, the Parthian capital. In February, 'laurelled despatches were sent to the senate by the emperor Trajan Augustus, on account of which he was named *Parthicus* ['conqueror of the Parthians']' (*AE* 1936, 97), and besides 'Parthia captured' the coins proclaimed that 'Armenia and Mesopotamia have been subjected to the power of the Roman people'.

The senate voted Trajan another triumph, but celebrations were premature, for, while he was still in the neighbourhood of Ctesiphon, the emperor learned that 'all of the conquered territories were in chaos and rebelling, and the garrisons of each of them

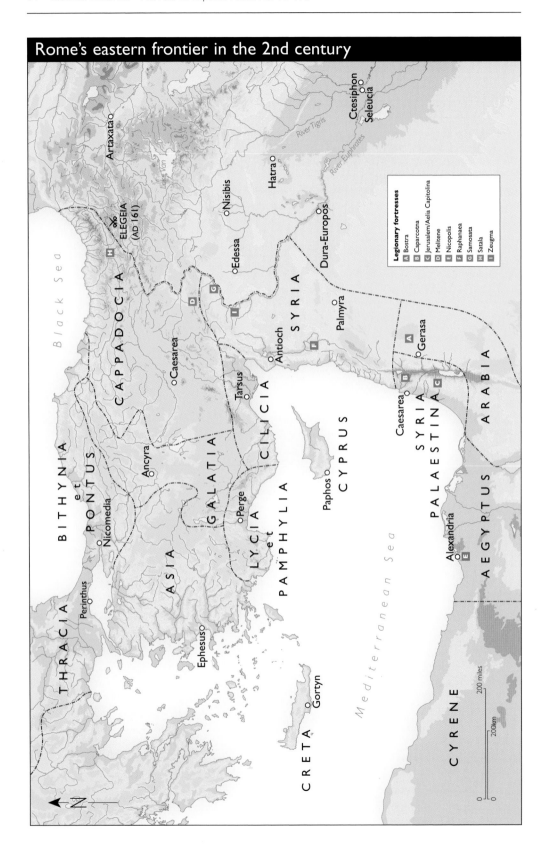

Rome's eastern frontier in the 2nd century

Legionary fortresses
A Bostra
B Caparcotna
C Jerusalem/Aelia Capitolina
D Melitene
E Nicopolis
F Raphanaea
G Samosata
H Satala
I Zeugma

had either been thrown out or slain' (Cassius Dio, *Roman History* 68.29.4). In an attempt to salvage the situation, a 'friendly king' was installed in Ctesiphon – the coinage even announces a 'King given to the Parthians' – and Lusius Quietus' Moors were unleashed on the unfortunate Nisibis and Edessa. But a Jewish revolt, perhaps originally sparked by Quietus' heavy-handedness, had quickly spread from Mesopotamia to Alexandria and beyond; it was no doubt for this reason that the tribune of the Seventh Claudia Legion, Gaius Valerius Rufus, was 'sent with a detachment by the Emperor Nerva Trajan Optimus Augustus Germanicus Dacicus Parthicus on the expedition to Cyprus' (*ILS* 9491). With the eastern frontier in flames, Trajan made his way back to Antioch for the winter.

The health of the emperor, who was by now over 60 years of age, began to fail, and

The River Euphrates near the location of the legionary fortress at Zeugma (Belkis in present-day Turkey), which has now been submerged beneath the flood waters of a new dam. The fortress name means 'The Bridge', because it controlled one of the key river crossings from the province of Syria into Parthia. (© Jona Lendering)

he was persuaded to return to Rome, but got no further than Cilicia (in southern Turkey) before dropping dead. In the meantime, although Hadrian was Trajan's closest living relative, the emperor had not made the succession clear. Hadrian's only consulship was as a relatively undistinguished *suffectus* in AD 108, and there were those who doubted the letter of adoption that he produced soon after Trajan's death. (Trajan's loyal generals Palma and Quietus perhaps objected, for they were almost immediately executed for treason.) However, Hadrian enjoyed the backing of Trajan's widow, whose influence ensured that he was nominated as ordinary consul for AD 118, and coins were rapidly issued proclaiming 'Hadrianus Trajanus Caesar'.

Imperial travels

Trajan was remembered as an ideal emperor; according to the writer Eutropius, the accession of later emperors was accompanied by the hope that they would be 'more fortunate than Augustus, more excellent

than Trajan' (*Breviarium* 8.5). Hadrian was cast in quite a different mould.

He began as he meant to continue. Although Arabia was retained, 'he relinquished everything beyond the Tigris and Euphrates ... [and] permitted the Armenians to have a king' (Augustan History, *Life of Hadrian* 5.3, 21.11). The provinces of Cappadocia and Galatia were once more separated. Dacia was reorganized into Dacia Superior and Dacia Inferior, shedding in the process an eastern tranche of land to the neighbouring Roxolani; soon after, a third division was made, creating the procuratorial province of Dacia Porolissensis in the north. This last decision had perhaps been prompted by the sudden and unexpected end to the dazzling career of Trajan's general Quadratus Bassus, who 'died while campaigning in Dacia and managing the province' (*AE* 1933, 268). Consular commands were becoming smaller;

Hadrian's Wall, looking east towards the location of the fort at Housesteads. The defensive character of the frontier wall is evident, as it runs along the crags.

no province now held more than three legions, and the largest garrison was now in Britain, cut off beyond the Channel and not easily reinforced in an emergency.

In that province, after the glorious achievements of the Flavians, the reign of Trajan had seen retreat and retrenchment, and the virtual abandonment of the area of present-day Scotland. Simmering trouble – not helped by Trajan's withdrawal of an entire legion, the Ninth Hispana (though some still argue for its destruction in Britain) – had erupted into open conflict near the beginning of Hadrian's reign, so he mounted a full-scale expedition, transferring the Sixth Victrix Legion from Germania Inferior to join the Second Augusta and Twentieth Valeria Victrix as the permanent garrison. His long-term solution, entrusted to the governor Aulus Platorius Nepos, was the building of the great stone frontier wall from Tyne to Solway that nowadays bears his name.

The Augustan History dryly notes that 'there were no important campaigns during

Milecastle 39 (Castle Nick) on Hadrian's Wall. The milecastles on Hadrian's Wall were the equivalent of fortlets elsewhere, designed to accommodate a small squad detached from their parent fort. Amongst the finds were several gaming boards, attesting to the long periods of inactivity along the frontier.

his reign, and wars were conducted almost without comment' (*Life of Hadrian* 21.8). On the contrary, Hadrian's reign was marked by reorganization and restructuring, as he travelled around his empire (the first emperor to do so), 'visiting the provinces and towns, and inspecting the garrisons and fortifications' (Cassius Dio, *Roman History* 69.9.1). First, in the early AD 120s, Hadrian visited Raetia, Noricum and the German provinces, reviewing the military installations and ordering the erection of a frontier barrier of massive wooden stakes. Then he moved on to Britain – the *expeditio Britannica* ('British expedition'), involving legionary detachments from Hispania Tarraconensis and Germania Superior, probably occurred now – after which he visited Spain and perhaps crossed over to Mauretania. From there, he travelled

to the eastern front, returning through Asia Minor to Greece, which held a special fascination for the philhellene emperor, and thence to Rome by mid-decade. After only a year or so, in AD 128, he set off once more on another tour of his empire, going first to Africa, where he famously addressed the men of the Third Augusta Legion at their fortress of Lambaesis, praising them for their efficient military drill – the writer Fronto scoffed that 'the army amused itself in camp with practice-weapons, instead of using real swords and shields' (*Preamble to History* 10) – and then visiting Greece again, before proceeding to the eastern front. He then returned via the Danubian provinces and was back in Rome in AD 134.

Some years before, he had ordered the construction of a new city called Aelia Capitolina on the ruins of Jerusalem, and the erection of a grand temple to Jupiter there. As if this were not insulting enough to the Jews, he seems also to have forbidden their tradition of circumcision, all of which met with a violent response. United under a leader known as Simon Bar Kochba ('the son of a star') and armed with weapons that their workshops had been commissioned to manufacture for the Roman army, insurgents created havoc throughout Judaea for four years (AD 132–35).

Cassius Dio records that 'Hadrian sent his best generals against them, foremost of whom was Sextus Julius Severus, sent against the Jews from Britain, where he was the governor' (*Roman History* 69.13.2). Unfortunately, we have no Josephus to describe this Second Jewish War for us, but it was clearly a bloody affair. By this stage, there were two legions in the province; the governor of Syria, Gaius Publicius Marcellus, brought a third, the Third Gallica, while the governor of Arabia, Titus Haterius Nepos, brought a fourth, the Third Cyrenaica; and reinforcements were summoned from Pannonia. The fact that 'when Hadrian wrote to the senate, he did not use the customary imperial preamble, "It is well if you and your children are in good health; I and my legions

The emperor Hadrian, wearing the *paludamentum* ('general's cloak') and protected by the *gorgoneion* ('Medusa face') on his cuirass. A famous philhellene, he set the fashion for subsequent emperors to wear the Greek-style beard. (Marie-Lan Nguyen-PD)

are in good health"' (Cassius Dio, *Roman History* 69.14.3) indicates the seriousness of the Roman losses. Emergency drafts were sent to keep the Tenth Fretensis Legion up to strength, and the Twenty-Second Deiotariana is thought to have been entirely destroyed, for it has left no traces after this time.

Eventually, the insurgents were besieged in the fortress of Bethar, where they were 'driven to the brink of destruction by hunger and thirst, and the instigator of the rebellion paid the penalty he deserved' (Eusebius, *Ecclesiastical History* 4.6.3). The victor, Julius Severus, was rewarded with *ornamenta triumphalia* 'for his successful actions in Judaea' (*ILS* 1056), but his subordinates – such as the African senator, Quintus Lollius Urbicus, who served as 'legate of the emperor Hadrian on the Judaean expedition' (*ILS* 1065) – received minimal military decorations. Despite taking an imperatorial acclamation (only his second and his last), Hadrian clearly wished to forget the whole affair. The province was even renamed Syria Palaestina.

Meanwhile, the governor of Cappadocia, Lucius Flavius Arrianus, was obliged to make preparations to repulse the Sarmatian Alani, who were threatening to invade Armenia and Mesopotamia. In the event, they were 'persuaded by gifts from Vologaeses [the Parthian king, Vologaeses III] and deterred by Flavius Arrianus, the governor of Cappadocia' (Cassius Dio, *Roman History* 69.15.1). The text of his *Battle Array against the Alans* survives, but it seems that he was never required to put it into operation.

A temporary emperor

Hadrian fell ill in AD 136, aged 60, and his thoughts turned to the succession. His intention was to groom the teenager Marcus Annius Verus (who came from good patrician stock) and his younger kinsman, later known as Lucius Verus, as joint heirs, so he adopted the wealthy 50-year-old Titus Aurelius Antoninus (later known as Antoninus Pius) as regent, instructing him to adopt the two boys as his own heirs. When Hadrian died in

AD 138, Antoninus Pius acceded to the throne without fuss. From the start, he singled Marcus out as his successor by giving him the new name Marcus Aurelius Caesar, and the two shared the ordinary consulship for AD 140, although Marcus was then only 18.

Antoninus Pius had followed the career of a patrician, holding the consulship at the age of 33 and proceeding (after a few posts in Italy) to the proconsulship of Asia in AD 134/35. He had never governed a frontier province; he had never even seen an army. Consequently, just like Domitian on his accession, he cast around for a likely theatre to provide him with much-needed military credibility, and just like Claudius, he decided upon Britain. However, unlike Domitian, he decided to remain in Rome, 'so that, being in a central location, he could rapidly receive news from every quarter' (Augustan History, *Life of Antoninus Pius* 7.12).

The new governor of Britannia, Lollius Urbicus, immediately began preparations for an advance into the Scottish lowlands, and victory had been won by AD 142. The Augustan History records that Antoninus 'defeated the Britons through his legate Lollius Urbicus, and another wall, this time of turf, was carried across, once the barbarians were cleared away' (*Life of Antoninus Pius* 5.4, referring to the Antonine Wall, which runs from the Forth to the Clyde in Scotland). It was remembered generations later that the emperor had won a war in Britain, 'although he had delegated command of it, while sitting in the city palace' (*Ancient Latin Panegyrics* 8 (5).14.2). No *ornamenta triumphalia* were awarded, but Antoninus took his second (and last) imperatorial acclamation and Urbicus went on to hold the prestigious role of *praefectus urbi*.

The orator Aelius Aristides wrote, 'So great is your peace, though war was traditional among the Romans' (*Roman Oration* 71a). However, all was not quiet during this 'golden period'. In later years, the writer Polyaenus, addressing Antoninus' successors, Marcus Aurelius and Lucius Verus, flattered them by claiming that 'alongside your father, you drew up plans to manage the conquered Moors, the subjugated Britons, and the humbled Getae' (*Stratagems* 6. Preface; the Getae were a branch of the Dacians, but their name is sometimes used loosely to indicate the entire people). The Augustan History also records how Antoninus 'forced the Moors to sue for peace, and crushed the Germans and the Dacians and many other tribes and also the rebellious Jews, through governors and legates' (*Life of Antoninus Pius* 5.4). There is no other record of Jewish trouble – indeed, such a conflict would be surprising, so soon after Hadrian's

The emperor Antoninus Pius, depicted in the costume of a Roman general, although this famously unmilitary man never left Italy during his 23-year reign. (Alinari via Getty Images)

The Roman fort at Hardknott (in Cumbria) was one of the Hadrianic bases that were evacuated around AD 139 to enable the advance into Scotland under Antoninus Pius. A heavily-buttressed granary building can be seen in the foreground. (© Jonathan Bailey/Arcaid/Corbis)

devastating war – and events on the Suebian German front seem rather to have taken the form of diplomacy, for the coinage proclaimed a 'King given to the Quadi'. However, there were serious wars against the Moors and the Dacians.

Throughout Antoninus' reign, trouble simmered in the two Mauretanias, occasionally bursting into full-scale war. In the later AD 140s, the equestrian Titus Varius Clemens, having completed his *tres militiae*, served as 'prefect of the auxiliary units sent from Hispania to Mauretania Tingitana' for the *expeditio in Tingitania* ('expedition to Tingitana'; *ILS* 1362); he received no military decorations, but rapid promotion followed as procurator of five different provinces, one after the other (including Mauretania Caesariensis and Raetia, both of which held large auxiliary armies). Similarly, auxiliary diplomas from the Danubian provinces, issued in

AD 150–51, refer to the discharge of troops 'when they were on the expedition to Mauretania Caesariensis' (*ILS* 9056).

There was also war in Dacia. In AD 156–58, the one-legion garrison of Dacia Superior, governed by Marcus Statius Priscus, was reinforced by 'detachments from Africa and Mauretania and Caesariensis, with Moorish tribesmen' (*ILS* 2006). Priscus subsequently erected a dedication to *Victoria Augusta* ('the emperor's victory'; *CIL* 3, 1416), a sure sign of successful warfare, along with an altar to Jupiter *optimus maximus*, 'for the welfare of the Roman empire and the courage of the Thirteenth Gemina Legion' (*ILS* 4006).

Success did not follow everywhere. By AD 158, the decision had been made to evacuate the Antonine Wall in Scotland, perhaps under increasing pressure from unruly tribes, and the governor Gnaeus Julius Verus began reinstating Hadrian's Wall as the northern frontier in Britain.

Embattled frontiers

The reign of Antoninus Pius had been welcomed as the bright noon, but his death in AD 161 brought only gathering gloom for his successors. No sooner had they paid the Praetorian Guard their now standard donative (20,000 sesterces per man) with the newly minted coinage proclaiming *felicitas temporum* ('the good fortune of the times') – Marcus was also celebrating the birth of his son Commodus – than trouble flared up on various fronts: 'at that time, there also came the Parthian War, which Vologaeses had prepared under Pius and declared under Marcus and Verus… War also threatened in Britain, and the Chatti had invaded Germany and Raetia' (Augustan History, *Life of Marcus Antoninus* 8.6–7).

In the east, in a replay of events under Trajan, the new Parthian king, Vologaeses IV, installed his own nominee on the throne of Armenia without Roman consultation.

Roman fort at Saalburg (near Bad Homburg, Germany), reconstructed in the 1890s after extensive excavations. The fort in its current form replaced an earlier Domitianic structure and dates from the reign of Antoninus Pius, whose statue stands outside the main south gate. (Ekem/PD)

The governor of neighbouring Cappadocia, Marcus Sedatius Severianus, foolishly took matters into his own hands and marched one of his legions into Armenia. Governors were not supposed to act without imperial instructions, particularly when it involved stepping beyond their own province, but a false oracle had promised that he would 'overpower Parthians and Armenians with your sharp spear' (Lucian, *Alexander* 27). Instead, the Parthians 'surrounded the entire legion under Severianus at Elegeia, a place in Armenia, and destroyed it along with its commanders by shooting them down from all sides' (Cassius Dio, *Roman History* 71.2.1). The legion may have been the Ninth Hispana, if it had survived this long.

From there, the Parthians invaded Syria and routed the governor's army in AD 162. The situation was clearly grave. Statius Priscus, earmarked for the British governorship, was diverted to Cappadocia, and Sextus Calpurnius Agricola was sent to Britannia in his place. Meanwhile, Gaius Aufidius Victorinus (Marcus' boon

companion and son-in-law of his tutor, Fronto) was sent to Germania Superior to deal with the Chatti. But the focus was firmly on the east, where the situation required the presence of an emperor. Marcus sent Lucius Verus. He took a leisurely course through Greece and around Asia Minor. Priscus probably took a more direct route, travelling with the expeditionary force, which comprised three entire legions (the First Minervia, the Second Adiutrix and the Fifth Macedonica).

Once in the war zone, Statius Priscus took a task force into Armenia and recaptured Artaxata; new coinage proclaiming 'a King given to the Armenians' accompanied the installation of a new Roman nominee. By the end of AD 163, Lucius Verus had taken the title *Armeniacus* ('conqueror of the Armenians'), and the two emperors received their second imperatorial acclamation. After a further year's preparations, a three-pronged punitive invasion of Mesopotamia was launched. One force under the command of Gaius Avidius Cassius, commander of the Third Gallica Legion, stormed and sacked the twin cities of Ctesiphon and Seleucia, although the inhabitants of the latter had opened their gates to the Romans.

The last action occurred early in AD 166. Both emperors were now IMP IV and both took the titles *Parthicus Maximus* ('greatest conqueror of the Parthians'). Although no *ornamenta triumphalia* were awarded, the main players received military decorations; for example, Marcus Claudius Fronto, commander of the First Minervia Legion, who had led one of the task forces in Mesopotamia, received *hastae purae quattuor*, *vexilla quattuor* ('four silver spears and four flags') and a selection of four gold crowns (*ILS* 1097–98). The emperors staged a grand triumph in autumn that year, the first such procession in living memory, and Marcus'

The so-called *decursio* (a circling funeral procession) from the base of the (now lost) red granite Column of Antoninus Pius, erected by Marcus Aurelius and Lucius Verus on the occasion of their adoptive father's apotheosis. The rider at the top is thought to represent either Marcus or Lucius. (UIG via Getty Images)

The emperor Lucius Verus, depicted in the costume of a Roman general. The sculpture on his cuirass represents the winged goddess Victoria, carrying a palm branch and olive wreath. A captive cowers beneath a trophy on either side, and the supine figure of a woman perhaps represents Armenia. (Alinari via Getty Images)

son was named Commodus Caesar. They may have hoped that the gloom had lifted, but it was about to descend again.

A plague (probably smallpox or typhus) had afflicted the inhabitants of Seleucia, from where it spread to the Roman invaders, and by AD 166 had cut great swathes through the Roman legions, travelling as far as the Rhine frontier and the city of Rome itself, with devastating effects (the famous medical writer Galen fled the city at this point). With catastrophic timing, the northern frontier now erupted into crisis, as the powerful Suebian tribes, pressed from the rear by migrating peoples, finally flexed their muscle. According to the Augustan History, 'for a long while they had been held in check by the diplomacy of the men on the spot, so that, once the eastern war had been concluded, the Marcomannic War could be waged' (*Life of Marcus Antoninus* 12.13).

The Column of Marcus Aurelius in the Piazza Colonna (Rome) was probably constructed to coincide with the emperor's triumph in AD 176, but may only have been completed after his death in AD 180. Like Trajan's Column, the 100ft structure was chiefly admired in antiquity for its internal spiral staircase, although it, too, has a sculptural frieze winding up the outside. (Arpingstone-PD)

Arrangements had already been made to raise two new legions, the Second and Third Italica, to restore the empire-wide total to 30. The raising of new legions had, in the past, heralded a desire to annex new territory; but, this time, Marcus was probably more concerned with meeting the increasing threat to the frontiers; in the event, the new legions were assigned to Raetia and Noricum. Simultaneously, the Dacian provinces were reunited and the new governor, Calpurnius Agricola, was given two legions. He is never heard of again. As the Augustan History notes, 'many nobles died in the German or Marcomannic War, or rather "the war of many tribes"' (*Life of Marcus Antoninus* 22.7).

Early in AD 167, the first of the Suebian tribes (Langobardi and Obii) burst across the frontier and were repelled by the Pannonian garrison, which hailed the emperors as

Above: Scene IX on the Column of Marcus Aurelius, showing the emperor's *adlocutio* ('address') to his troops, probably at the beginning of the campaign of AD 172. (Simone Ramella/CC-BY-2.0)

Below: Scene XVI on the Column of Marcus Aurelius, showing a column of weary soldiers, worn out by thirst, being miraculously refreshed by the so-called 'Rain Miracle'. Soldiers in charge of a mule cart (perhaps transporting a catapult) shelter beneath their shields as the rain lashes down. (Simone Ramella/CC-BY-2.0)

imperator for the fifth time. In the following year, 'the two emperors set out wearing their generals' cloaks' (Augustan History, *Life of Marcus Antoninus* 14.1); their *consilium* included those of the great generals who had survived the plague. When they crossed the Alps, it was the first time Marcus had stepped beyond Italy. The two new legions now took up position in defence of Italy under

The emperor Marcus Aurelius, dressed in the costume of a general and surrounded by soldiers, displays his *clementia* ('mercy') to two kneeling barbarians. (De Agostini/Getty Images)

Quintus Antistius Adventus (a decorated commander in the *expeditio Parthica*, 'Parthian expedition', and a future governor of Britannia). However, Lucius Verus soon succumbed to the plague and Marcus was obliged to return to Rome for his funeral.

It was AD 170 before he finally reached the northern frontier, where he directed a massive, but ultimately disastrous, offensive against the Suebian tribes. The victorious Marcomanni and Quadi rampaged through Noricum to northern Italy, where they besieged Aquileia. Further east, other tribes (including the Costoboci) ranged through the Balkans, plundering as far as Greece. This sector had been entrusted to Claudius Fronto, highly decorated in the Parthian War, who 'after several battles against the Germans and Jazyges, finally fell fighting vigorously for the Republic' (*ILS* 1098). In the following year, the Marcomanni were halted at the Danube as they tried to carry

their booty home. Marcus finally took his sixth imperatorial acclamation, and the coinage (somewhat optimistically) proclaimed a *Victoria Germanica* ('victory over the Germans').

Cassius Dio notes depressingly that 'the emperor himself fought for a long time (almost his whole life, it could be said) against the barbarians along the Danube, both Jazyges and Marcomanni, one after the other, from his base in Pannonia' (*Roman History* 71.3.1). The base was now moved to the fortress at Carnuntum (25 miles downriver from Vienna), and Marcus opened negotiations with the Marcomanni. Simultaneously, his military secretary and future *praefectus praetorio*, Publius Tarrutienus Paternus, attempted to make an alliance with the Cotini, a minor tribe bordering the Quadi, but was rebuffed. The tribes continued to be restless and unpredictable.

Another massive offensive was mounted in AD 172, and after hard fighting the Marcomanni were defeated (with the aid of the supernatural 'lightning and rain miracle', depicted on the Column of Marcus Aurelius in Rome); Marcus and the 11-year-old Commodus both took the title of *Germanicus* ('conqueror of the Germans'). In the following year (in which Marcus began writing his famous *Meditations*), attention turned to the Quadi and their allies, the Naristae, whose chieftain was killed by the equestrian Marcus Valerius Maximianus. Having settled the Quadi, the campaign of AD 174 was directed against the Jazyges, during which Marcus was able to take a seventh imperatorial acclamation, but the Quadi revolted and expelled the 'friendly king' whom Marcus had given them.

Just as the campaigning season opened in AD 175, news arrived that Avidius Cassius had declared himself emperor in Syria. As a loyal and highly decorated general, his rebellion continues to baffle historians, but he was perhaps misled by spurious reports of Marcus' death. The emperor was obliged to make peace with the Jazyges in order to deal with this new crisis, but loyal agents in Syria took matters into their own hands, and

Figure of a triumphant general, thought to be
the emperor Lucius Verus, on a relief from Ephesus.
(© Jona Lendering)

Cassius 'was killed after dreaming of empire
for only three months and six days' (Cassius
Dio, *Roman History* 71.27.3). Meanwhile, the
Romans had managed to get the upper hand
on the northern frontier, so that Marcus
felt justified in taking an eighth acclamation,
along with the title *Sarmaticus* ('conqueror of
the Sarmatians'), and, late in the following
year, the spirits of the Roman populace were
raised by the staging of a grand triumph.

However, the northern frontier was
not yet at peace. Marcus had taken a ninth
imperatorial acclamation in AD 177 (this
was Commodus' second, as the teenager
was now joint emperor), indicating that
the campaigning continued; father and son
travelled to the frontier in the following year
for the *expeditio Germanica secunda* ('second
German expedition'). A victory won by
Paternus enabled Marcus to take a tenth
imperatorial acclamation (Commodus'
third), and Roman troops were now

stationed in force throughout enemy
territory. A well-known rock-cut inscription
from Trenčin (Hungary), in the heartlands
of the Quadi, carries a dedication to *Victoria
Augustorum* ('The emperors' victory'; *ILS*
9122) by 'the army based at Leugaricio',
which apparently included the Second
Adiutrix Legion under Valerius Maximianus,
the 'commander of the detachments
wintering at Leugaricio' (*AE* 1956, 124).
Cassius Dio records that the soldiers
'had bathhouses and all the necessities in
abundance' (*Roman History* 71.20.1), and
we might imagine that, by AD 179, the area
had been pacified to a similar extent as
Germania Magna in AD 9. In fact, the
Augustan History even suggests that Marcus
'wished to make a province of Marcomannia
and also Sarmatia, and would have done so,
if Avidius Cassius had not rebelled in the
east' (*Life of Marcus Antoninus* 24.5). But,
where the *clades Variana* brought an end to
Augustus' plans for a province beyond the
Rhine, Marcus' plans – if they were genuine –
were spoiled, not by Cassius, but by his
son Commodus.

Gaius Velius Rufus

One of the main avenues of social mobility in the Roman empire was provided by the legionary centurionate. Men who were successful in this role – or who could count upon powerful patronage – might hope to reach the coveted position of *primus pilus* ('chief centurion'), in charge (for one year only) of the first cohort of the legion. This cohort, according to the late military writer Vegetius (*Epitome of Military Matters* 2.6.2), 'looks after the *aquila* ["eagle totem"], which has always been the principal standard of the Roman army and the ensign of the entire legion; and it worships the images of the emperors, which are the divine and pre-eminent *signa* ["battle-standards"]'.

After their one-year stint, those who did not simply retire with their generous cash bonus might hope to exploit their new equestrian status as *primipilares* ('men who had been *primus pilus*'), for a whole new selection of posts now opened up before them. For those who were wedded to life on the frontiers, the highly respected position of *praefectus castrorum* in a legion beckoned. Otherwise, rather than the command of an auxiliary unit – which, since at least the reign of Claudius, had been the prerogative of the equestrian gentleman – there was a round of the more prestigious tribunates at Rome (in the *vigiles*, *urbaniciani* and *praetoriani*), after which the *primipilaris* was free to compete with the equestrians for one of the highly paid procuratorships.

Our knowledge of Roman careers (whether they relate to humble legionaries or to the most distinguished consulars) derives mostly from inscriptions, for the Romans had an 'epigraphic habit' – a predilection for immortalizing their successes in stone. The habit grew over the course of the 1st century, reaching a peak towards the end of the second. Near the mid-point of this

process, an epitaph (published as *ILS* 9200) was erected in the Roman town of Heliopolis (modern Baalbek in Lebanon), celebrating the eventful career of the *primipilaris* Gaius Velius Rufus.

It was usual for a man's heir to arrange for his commemoration. In Rufus' case, this was Marcus Alfius Olympiacus, veteran *aquilifer* ('eagle bearer') of the Fifteenth Apollinaris, a Pannonian legion that had been sent east by Nero and had seen service in the Jewish War, before being shipped back to its fortress at Carnuntum. The eagle-bearers stood apart from the usual hierarchy of legionary officers. Like the centurions, they were long-service soldiers, whom only death or retirement could remove from their post, and each one enjoyed great respect as the keeper of the *aquila*, a duty that they shared with the annually changing *primus pilus*.

Rufus' epitaph, like the epitaphs of other *primipilares*, does not detail his previous career. However, we can imagine that – in common with many other centurions – he had dotted from legion to legion, criss-crossing the Mediterranean world and accumulating years of experience, at some stage surely serving alongside Olympiacus in the Fifteenth Apollinaris.

In fact, their acquaintance may date back to the Jewish War, when Rufus received *dona militaria* ('military decorations') for heroic conduct. His epitaph lists the standard *torques phalerae armillae* ('collars, decorative discs and bracelets') along with the gold crown (in this case, the *corona vallaris*, 'rampart crown'), which was an appropriate set of decorations for a centurion (ordinary legionaries received less, *primipilares* expected more). Distinguished service might also mark a man out for advancement (although the precise ranking of legionary centurions is still poorly understood). Another centurion

The epitaph of Gaius Velius Rufus (*ILS* 9200), discovered in the courtyard of the Temple of Jupiter at Baalbek (Lebanon), was probably erected during the reign of Trajan. Although Rufus twice received military decorations from Domitian, the inscription tactfully avoids mentioning that emperor's name. (© Jona Lendering)

similarly decorated in the Jewish War, Marcus Blossius Pudens, had fallen at the last hurdle: 'he paid his debt to nature [i.e. he died] almost on the day of becoming *primus pilus*' (*ILS* 2641). He was 49 years old (roughly the norm for *primipilares*).

Olympiacus, having listed the various highlights of Rufus' career, saves the best (or, at any rate, the most historically significant) till last. 'Having been sent to Parthia', runs the text of the epitaph, 'he escorted Epiphanes and Callinicus, the sons of King Antiochus, back to the emperor Vespasian, along with a large band of men who were liable for the payment of tribute'. We know that, following the annexation of Commagene in AD 72, its king, Antiochus, had surrendered himself to Vespasian, but his sons had fled to the court of the Parthian king. However, when they saw that their father was being humanely (even luxuriously) treated, they agreed to join him in Rome. The arrangements must have entailed the kind of diplomatic work often reserved for legionary centurions. Corbulo, for example, had communicated with the Parthian king using, as intermediary, one of the legionary centurions on the spot, so it would have been natural for Vespasian to do likewise.

Success in this task must have marked Rufus out for future rewards, for which he was, perhaps, as yet too young. His epitaph jumps ahead to the coveted post of *primus pilus* in the Twelfth Fulminata Legion, based in Cappadocia. Unfortunately, the date is unknown, but his first post as a *primipilaris*, the tribunate of the Thirteenth Urban Cohort (a prestigious post equivalent to the usual three tribunates at Rome, because this cohort uniquely lay at Carthage), fell early in Domitian's reign. It was no doubt towards the end of Rufus' tenure of this post that trouble broke out in the neighbouring Mauretanias. Presumably, the commander of the Third Augusta Legion could not respond because he was engaged in exterminating the Nasamones, an event that occurred around AD 85. Furthermore, it seems that a new tribune had been sent to bring the Thirteenth Urban Cohort to the Danube front. Certainly,

a centurion of the cohort, Quintus Vilanius Nepos, was decorated 'by Domitian for the Dacian War, and again by him for the German War, and again with torques and bracelets for the Dacian War' (*ILS* 2127).

With the African legion unavailable, Rufus was put in charge of a composite force, as 'commander of the African and Mauretanian army with the task of suppressing the tribes in Mauretania'. Nothing further is known of this war, but Rufus must have acquitted himself well, as he received another set of decorations, this time appropriate to his status as a *primipilaris*: namely, *hastae duae*, *vexilla duo* ('twin silver spears and twin flags') and a gold crown (in this case, the *corona muralis*, 'battlemented crown'). Victory in Mauretania must have drawn him to the attention of Domitian (or his *consilium*), and he soon found himself in command of a legionary battlegroup on the Danube front (the inscription lists 'detachments from nine [*sic*] legions: the First Adiutrix, Second Adiutrix, Second Augusta, Eighth Augusta, Ninth Hispana, Fourteenth Gemina, Twentieth Victrix, Twenty-First Rapax'). Rufus again rose to the occasion, and 'in the war against the Marcomanni, Quadi and Sarmatians, against whom he made an expedition through the kingdom of Decebalus, King of the Dacians, he was decorated with the battlemented crown, twin silver spears and twin flags'.

The number of legions that participated or sent detachments for this campaign in AD 89 hints at the growing severity of the situation in the north. However, Rufus' military successes now justified the reward of a procuratorial career. First, he served as financial procurator of Dalmatia and Pannonia (to 'assist' their consular governors), and then as praesidial procurator of Raetia, a frontier province with a substantial auxiliary garrison. If Rufus survived (he might not yet have reached 60 years of age), his career, so closely bound up with the hated Domitian, perhaps faltered; or he may simply have retired from imperial service. But his friend Olympiacus ensured that what he achieved in life continued to echo in eternity, in the ruins at Baalbek.

Travels in an unarmed province

At some point during the reign of Antoninus Pius or his successors, the north African writer Apuleius wrote a novel entitled *Metamorphoses* (better known as *The Golden Ass*), which gives us a unique (if melodramatic) insight into ordinary provincial life. Apuleius took as his central theme a well-known Greek tale in which the hero, Lucius (Apuleius' own name), drinks a magic potion that transforms him into an ass; after various adventures, and having endured several different owners, Lucius manages to eat the antidote, a rose, and is turned back into human form.

The backdrop to the novel is the province of Macedonia, one of the so-called 'unarmed' senatorial provinces of the empire, administered by an annually appointed proconsul. Although not one of the emperor's legates, he was nevertheless entrusted with one or two auxiliary units to assist in keeping the peace. However, Macedonia was a large province, and, when Lucius (still in human form) visits the town of Hypata, he is warned not to stay out too late, because 'you may see murder victims lying in the middle of the street, for the governor's auxiliaries are far-off and cannot rid the town of such carnage' (*The Golden Ass* 2.18). In the novel, the town's troublemakers are a rabble of upper-class youths, who are free to make mischief in the absence of any sort of police force.

The countryside held its own dangers. Banditry was rife in the Roman empire, so much so that it was classified as a hazard of everyday life, along with earthquakes and floods. Military law laid down that a soldier returning late from leave was considered to be a deserter, unless he had been unavoidably delayed by illness or detained by bandits. In the novel, no sooner is Lucius transformed into an ass than he is taken by a local gang of bandits and loaded with stolen goods. When the townsfolk finally get the better of the bandits, they mete out summary justice, throwing some over a cliff and beheading the others. (The so-called Cornelian Law forbade the carrying of weapons 'for the purpose of murder or robbery', but there were no authorities on hand to exercise that law.) Like the inhabitants of many other small towns, they would probably see the provincial governor once a year, on his judicial tour; wrongdoers might be locked up in prison to await trial at that time, or the townsfolk might simply take matters into their own hands.

In times of serious trouble, the proconsul relied upon the assistance of his more powerful colleagues governing the neighbouring imperial provinces. For example, during Marcus Aurelius' northern wars, the equestrian Gaius Julius Vehilius Gratus was appointed as 'commander of the detachments in Greece and Macedonia opposing the Costoboci' (*ILS* 1327) who were ravaging the peninsula, and a little later, the highly decorated war hero Marcus Valerius Maximianus, while procurator of Moesia Inferior, was appointed 'commander of the detachments sent by the emperor to remove a band of Brisean bandits from the borders of Macedonia and Thrace' (*AE* 1956, 124).

The increasing warfare on the Danube and Euphrates was inevitably felt in the Balkans, through which troops marched on their way to the east, and echoed down into the Greek peninsula. In preparation for Trajan's Second Dacian War, the First Equitate Cohort of Spaniards, normally part of the garrison of Moesia Inferior, had its headquarters temporarily based at Stobi (present-day Gradsko in Macedonia), a hub from which the Adriatic, Aegean, Black Sea and Danube were all equally accessible for transport and communications. A papyrus (conventionally known as 'Hunt's *pridianum*', the technical term for a military strength report) lists the

Roman relief of a provincial family in travelling attire, discovered at Stobi (present-day Gradsko) in Macedonia. Both men carry wooden staves for protection, and the child wears a one-piece hooded cloak, known as a *birrus*. Such characters would not have been out of place in Apuleius' *The Golden Ass*. (Dave Proffer/CC-BY-2.0)

whereabouts of the cohort's 596 men: one had died by drowning; another had been 'killed by bandits'; others were 'in Gaul to collect clothing'; while a task force comprising a centurion, a decurion, 23 cavalrymen and two infantrymen earning pay-and-a-half were 'across the Danube on an expedition'.

It is not surprising, then, that one of the characters whom the asinine Lucius meets, after he has escaped from the bandits, is a soldier, who claims (fraudulently) that he needs the ass 'to carry the governor's baggage, alongside other pack animals, from a nearby fort' (*The Golden Ass* 9.39). The creature's current owner, a vegetable grower, cannot understand the soldier's Latin, for Greek was the lingua franca in the Balkans and the east, so he receives a blow from the soldier's staff. However, not wishing to hand over the ass, the vegetable grower sets about the soldier and makes off with his sword. The loss of a side-arm was a serious matter – the soldier would at least be required to purchase a new one – so he appeals to the town authorities, who arrest the vegetable grower, and the soldier appropriates the ass for his own use.

The arrogance and brutality of the soldiery were proverbial. The philosopher Epictetus famously advised, 'if a soldier takes your mule, let it go. Do not resist and do not complain. For, if you do, you will get a

beating and lose your mule all the same' (*Discourses* 4.1.79). In theory, there was a requisition system in operation, but provincial governors were periodically obliged to clamp down on abuses. A well-known bilingual edict issued by Sextus Sotidius Libuscidianus, the emperor Tiberius' governor of Galatia, laid down that 'the people of Sagalassus must provide a service of ten wagons and as many mules for the necessary use of people passing through, and should receive, from those who use the service, 2½ sesterces per *schoenum* for a wagon and 1 sesterce per *schoenum* for a mule … they are obliged to provide transport as far as Cormasa and Conana', which lay between 20 and 35 miles away (*AE* 1976, 653; the *schoenum* was an Asian measure of distance).

Of course, this kind of edict would not have helped Apuleius' vegetable grower, as his soldier was plainly acting beyond the law. To try and combat this kind of thuggish behaviour, the emperor Trajan's philosophy was to keep the soldiers out of mischief as far as possible: 'let us stick to the general rule', he wrote to Pliny the Younger, 'that as few soldiers as possible should be called away from the battle-standards' (*Letters* 10.20.2).

Apuleius' soldier subsequently sells the ass, because he has been sent to Rome as a messenger carrying a letter to the emperor. He thus makes a tidy profit of 44 sesterces from the sale, equivalent to around two weeks' pay for a legionary. The episode underlines the fact that, even in backwoods Macedonia, the provincials operated a cash economy. When Lucius first arrives in Hypata, he attempts to buy some fish at the market, and, by haggling, beats the fishmonger down to 80 sesterces – they must have been fine fish!

Apuleius' novel leaves us with the impression that, while history revolves around the emperor as the centre of attention at Rome or on his travels, and a select band of his senatorial and equestrian colleagues rose through the ranks doing the emperor's bidding, life continued at a different pace in the 'unarmed' provinces, where folk were mostly oblivious to the great events on the frontiers.

Dio Cocceianus 'Chrysostom'

The life of the intellectual Dio Cocceianus is roughly contemporary with Velius Rufus' military career. His full name is unknown, but he may have been a Tiberius Claudius, if his family – as is suspected – owed their citizenship to the emperor Claudius. His persuasive prose style, displayed in a series of 80 so-called *Orations* on a variety of subjects, earned him the posthumous nickname *Chrysostom*, 'golden mouth'. Both Rufus and Dio ultimately came to Domitian's notice, but where one benefited from the emperor's attention and (as we have seen) increased in status, the other fell foul of the tyrant's paranoia.

Dio was born in the small Bithynian town of Prusa (present-day Bursa in north-western Turkey) some time around AD 40 (making him contemporary with the emperor Titus). As a Greek intellectual, he naturally dabbled in local politics, but as a member of the landed gentry, he also rubbed shoulders with the rich and powerful. In his seventh oration (known as the *Euboean*), he claims that 'I knew the homes and tables of rich men, not only private individuals, but governors and emperors' (*Orations* 7.66). The identification is controversial, but it seems likely that Dio's 'emperors' were the three members of the Flavian dynasty.

The writer Philostratus claims that Dio was on hand in Alexandria (along with the philosopher Apollonius of Tyana) when Vespasian made his bid for empire in AD 69, and that Dio even gave him advice, namely that he should crush Vitellius' regime before it could become established. Some have argued that Dio's 30-second oration (the *Alexandrian*) was delivered in the city at around this time, for the writer refers to recent troubles there that may have stemmed from the First Jewish War.

The Egyptian capital was notorious for the volatility of its mixed Greek and Jewish population, and disagreements often erupted into rioting. It was chiefly for this reason that Augustus had assigned two legions to the city (the Third Cyrenaica and Twenty-Second Deiotariana). In AD 74, the Roman siege of Masada, finally ending the First Jewish War, sparked a southward exodus of insurgents, who began to foment discontent in Alexandria. The incoming *praefectus Aegypti*, Tiberius Julius Lupus, was instructed by the emperor to demolish the Jewish Temple at Leontopolis, presumably to remove a potential focus of unrest while advertising Roman ruthlessness in restoring order.

In his *Alexandrian* oration, Dio informs us that the province's excellent Roman governors are forced to be suspicious of the population, not because they might revolt against Rome, but because of the unrest that might flare up unexpectedly. Dio notes that, 'in the disturbance that occurred [in the city], most of you expressed your rebellion verbally, and a few threw whatever came to hand once or twice, like those who shower slops on passers-by, and then settled down to chant or went down to the harbours, as if they were carousing at a festival' (*Orations* 32.71). Even then, 'the most excellent Conon' (could Dio mean Lucius Peducaeus Colon, Lupus' immediate predecessor as *praefectus Aegypti*?) was obliged to deploy his troops, and, although he planned only a show of force, 'the reckless and undisciplined elements, deceitfully trying to overturn everything and create chaos, would not let up until you'd had a taste of warfare and the danger had escalated to the limit' (*ibid.* 72). The city saw further disturbances under Trajan and Hadrian.

Another of Dio's orations (the forty-sixth), delivered to the citizens of Prusa, gives us an insight into how fragile a town's economy might be. It seems that, during a period of

shortage, the price of grain had skyrocketed. The town council first accused Dio of stockpiling in order to profit from the shortage, and then attempted to bully him into purchasing wheat for public distribution. Dio points out to them that his farms produce wine and cattle, not wheat, and that he has already performed benefactions for the city, although there are citizens far wealthier than he is. He deplores their threat of violence and fire-raising (a mob had already been turned back from his estate) and makes his own threat in return: 'far better to be an emigrant and take up residence in a foreign land than to be subjected to this kind of treatment' (*Orations* 46.12). The oration gives us an insight into small town life, and particularly into the importance of benefactions and patronage.

Dio's thirty-first oration (known as the *Rhodian*) was probably delivered at roughly the same time that Rufus was receiving *dona militaria* for his role in the First Jewish War and Jerusalem's ruins had been ground beneath the military boots of the Tenth Fretensis Legion. Dio's subject seems altogether more frivolous, as he denounces the citizens of Rhodes for the cynical recycling of honorific statues 'after the previous inscription has been erased and another name engraved' (*Orations* 31.9); how cunning, as it saves the expense of a new statue, but how dishonourable, as the mutilation of a statue and the erasure of a name symbolized disgrace. Dio also sings the praises of Rhodian freedom and criticizes the citizens for worrying that they might lose this coveted status – ironically, as not long after, the emperor Vespasian promptly cancelled the tax immunity that the philhellene Nero had granted to the island city!

Having been a friend of the Flavians, Dio's fortunes abruptly changed not long after

The Greek and Jewish communities of Egypt, Cyrene and the Levant had a history of sporadic violence. This Roman milestone from the province of Cyrene, erected in AD 118, records that Hadrian 'rebuilt the road, which was torn up and shattered in the Jewish revolt' (*AE* 1951, 208), referring to the disturbances sparked by Trajan's Parthian War. (sodabottle/CC-BY-SA-3.0)

Domitian came to power. Dio states that 'it so happened that I was exiled on account of my alleged friendship with a man who was not a rogue, but was prosperous and very close to those in power, and who was killed for those things that made him seem fortunate to nearly everyone, namely his connections by blood and marriage with those same people' (*Orations* 13.1). Dio does not name this friend, but it seems likely that he means Titus Flavius Sabinus, grandson of Vespasian's brother and hence Domitian's closest surviving relative; he was also the husband of Titus' daughter (Domitian's niece) Julia. As Domitian's consular colleague in AD 81, Sabinus had allegedly been announced, by mistake, as *imperator*; this was perhaps sufficient reason for the insecure emperor ('who was called master and god by all the Greeks and barbarians, but was really a wicked demon': *Orations* 45.1) to order his murder soon afterwards, and the removal of any supporters.

Dio's exile took him far and wide, 'without even a single servant' (*Orations* 40.2), and he was obliged to labour for a living. However, he found time to write a treatise on the Dacians, which unfortunately has not survived, though the writer Philostratus confirms that 'when he wandered as an outcast, he did indeed journey to the Getae' (*Lives of the Sophists* 487). Indeed, from the twelfth oration (known as the *Olympic*, as it was delivered to a crowd at Olympia in Greece, possibly at the Olympic games of AD 97), it appears that Dio was a witness to Dacian preparations for war: 'I have just come on a long journey from the Danube and the lands of the Getae', he says, '... as a peaceful observer of war ... desiring to see men contending like athletes, on the one hand for empire and influence, on the other hand for freedom and fatherland' (*Orations* 12.16, 19, 20). Even in the closing years of Domitian's reign, the Moesian frontier remained on high alert.

When word of Domitian's assassination in AD 96 was broadcast, Dio was present at a legionary fortress on the Danube, presumably the base of one of the Moesian legions, being nearest Dacia, so either Singidunum or Viminacium (Belgrade and Kostolac in present-day Serbia). He could not resist haranguing the troops on the tyrant's many faults. Intriguingly, it seems that the soldiers were on the verge of mutiny – had they heard rumours of Nigrinus' intentions in Syria? – but Dio advised them 'to make common cause with the Roman people' (*ibid.* 488).

The precise nature of Dio's exile has been debated. He had clearly been forbidden to visit Prusa, but his estate there had not been confiscated, for he was able to return to it on Domitian's death, although it had become ruinous from years of neglect. On Nerva's accession, Dio set out for Rome, but illness hindered his progress, and, on Nerva's death soon after, he was thus 'robbed of a benevolent emperor who was fond of me, and an old friend' (*Orations* 45.2). It seems that Dio had previously made Nerva's acquaintance, but the circumstances of their meeting remain unknown. (The theory that he owed his surname Cocceianus to Nerva, whose family name was Cocceius, has little to recommend it.)

On Dio's return to Prusa, he resumed his role as patron and benefactor, and received further honours from the townsfolk. He evidently led an embassy to Trajan, seeking the new emperor's favour, but his so-called *Kingship* orations – although addressed to an emperor who 'reviews an army, subdues a province, founds a city, bridges rivers and builds roads' (*Orations* 3.127), thus clearly Trajan – show no sign of the close relationship that he had evidently enjoyed with Nerva. During this period, the citizens of Asia Minor were gradually being integrated into high Roman politics (Quadratus Bassus, for example, a leading citizen of Pergamon, began his career under the Flavians and rose to be one of Trajan's *amici*), but Dio's politics did not extend beyond Prusa, and he essentially observes the Roman empire as an outsider.

Neglecting the empire

The gladiator emperor

Marcus Aurelius fell ill and died in spring AD 180. The automatic accession of the 18-year-old Commodus (who immediately became IMP IV), as far as Cassius Dio was concerned, transformed the Roman empire 'from a kingdom of gold to one of iron and rust' (*Roman History* 71.36.4). Not wishing to catch his father's illness, Commodus quickly concluded matters on the frontier, and hastened back to Rome to celebrate an undeserved triumph. Fundamentally uninterested in politics, he easily fell under the influence of his unscrupulous *praefectus praetorio* Sextus Tigidius Perennis (who saw to the removal of his sometime colleague, Paternus) and his successor, the even more deceitful Marcus Aurelius Cleander, and his reign was punctuated by conspiracies and executions. He was obsessed with gladiatorial combat, to the extent that he fought in the arena himself, and latterly became convinced that he was Hercules.

Cassius Dio reports that Commodus 'also had some wars with the barbarians beyond Dacia, in which both Albinus and Niger distinguished themselves, but the greatest war was the British one' (*Roman History* 72.8.1). The affairs in Dacia during these years are entirely unknown, and it may be that the two men whom Dio mentions, Decimus Clodius Albinus and Gaius Pescennius Niger, were governors in Moesia and Dacia. However, in Britain, tribes reportedly crossed Hadrian's Wall and killed a commander, perhaps the legate of the Sixth Victrix Legion at York. The governor Marcus Ulpius Marcellus crushed the invasion, but his iron discipline caused a mutiny. While Marcellus' career does not seem to have been harmed (he later obtained the coveted proconsulship of Asia), the province remained in an unsettled condition. Nevertheless, Commodus took two imperatorial acclamations in AD 183 and began styling himself *Britannicus* ('conqueror of the Britons') in the following year.

As the garrison of Britannia was openly mutinous, Commodus eventually called Publius Helvius Pertinax out of retirement and sent him to govern the province. Pertinax had served out his *militia equestris* ('equestrian military service') under Antoninus Pius and Marcus Aurelius before

Replica of the famous 11ft bronze equestrian statue of Marcus Aurelius, in the Piazza del Campidoglio (Rome). Rather than presenting a triumphalist image, the emperor's pose, unarmed and unarmoured, emphasizes his clemency. (Jastrow-PD)

being rewarded with senatorial status, enabling him to govern several important provinces, until the baleful influence of Perennis forced his retirement in AD 182. The fact that the troops in Britain wished Pertinax to become emperor – though he declined – may have put the thought into his mind, because he readily joined the conspiracy that successfully removed Commodus on the last day of AD 192, and became emperor in his place, another Galba to Commodus' Nero. Three months later, the *praetoriani* had killed him, too, and the Roman world again descended into civil war.

The emperor Commodus, in the guise of the demigod Hercules. A keen gladiatorial fighter, his growing megalomania caused him to neglect the administration of the empire, undoing much of the good work of his father and (adoptive) grandfather. (De Agostini/Getty Images)

A changing empire

For almost a century, the Roman empire had remained within its original boundaries. The great rivers of the Rhine, Danube and Euphrates continued to mark the limit of directly administered territory, and Augustus would not have criticized his successors for

occasionally imposing their will on the neighbouring peoples, purely in the interests of security. Only in Britain had Claudius' desire for military glory caused Augustus' advice to be ignored. Elsewhere, even if one-time 'friendly kingdoms' had become formal provinces, these were areas that Augustus had treated as part and parcel of the empire, in any case. Instead of volunteering gifts, they were now directly taxed; instead of supplying allied troops, their manpower was now conscripted into the Roman army.

By the reign of Domitian, the focus of attention had shifted decisively to the Danube, where repeated campaigning succeeded in maintaining the empire within the borders recommended by the first emperor, while projecting Roman authority beyond them. Pliny the Younger complained that, in Domitian's senate, 'we discussed massive triumphal arches and excessive inscriptions for the pediments of temples, as if the boundaries of the empire had been extended' (*Panegyric to Trajan* 54.4). This is unfair criticism. Slight inroads had been made in Germania Magna ('greater Germany' beyond the Rhine), where Domitian had embraced the fertile Wetterau region (around modern-day Frankfurt), but nothing to match Augustus' province-in-the-making that the *clades Variana* had lost.

Frontinus claims that, during his Chattan War, Domitian 'changed the method of warfare by creating over 120 miles of military roads' (*Stratagems* 1.3.10). The word that he uses for a military road – *limes* – soon acquired a new meaning, and is more familiar nowadays as the technical Latin term for a frontier. However, Domitian had no more thoughts of limiting his empire behind frontiers than Augustus had. His *limites* (the plural form of *limes*) on the Rhine were intended to open

The grandiose Arch of Septimius Severus, erected in AD 203, stamped the authority of the new Severan dynasty on Rome. Its scale stands in stark contrast to the smaller and less ornate Arch of Titus, at the opposite end of the Forum Romanum. The sculptured panels depict the successes of Severus' army in extending the empire into Mesopotamia. (Jean-Christophe Benoist/CC-BY-3.0)

The Roman world under Septimius Severus

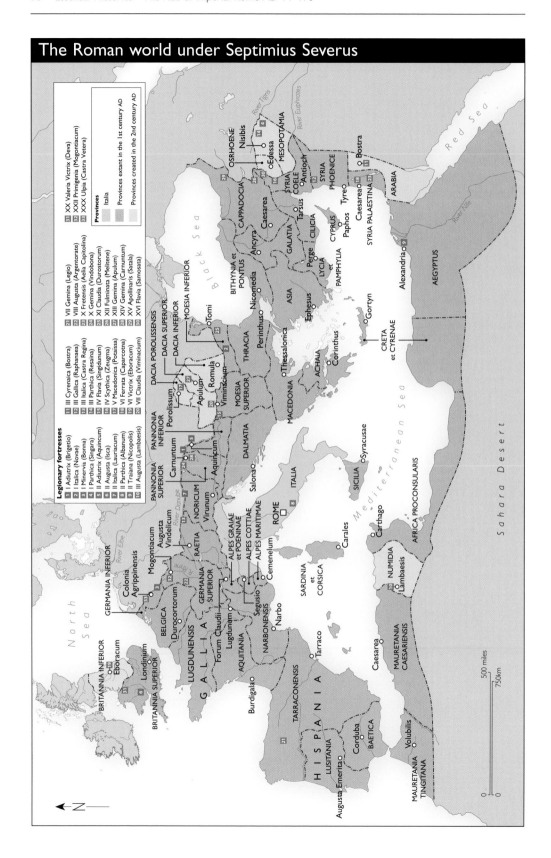

Legionary fortresses

1 I Adiutrix (Brigetio)
2 I Italica (Novae)
3 I Minervia (Bonna)
4 I Parthica (Singara)
5 II Adiutrix (Aquincum)
6 II Augusta (Isca)
7 II Italica (Lauriacum)
8 II Parthica (Albanum)
9 II Traiana (Nicopolis)
10 III Augusta (Lambaesis)

11 III Cyrenaica (Bostra)
12 III Gallica (Raphaneae)
13 III Italica (Castra Regina)
14 III Parthica (Resaina)
15 IV Flavia (Singidunum)
16 IV Scythica (Zeugma)
17 V Macedonica (Potaissa)
18 VI Ferrata (Caparcotna)
19 VI Victrix (Eboracum)
20 VII Claudia (Viminacium)

21 VII Gemina (Legio)
22 VIII Augusta (Argentorate)
23 X Fretensis (Aelia Capitolina)
24 X Gemina (Vindobona)
25 XI Claudia (Durostorum)
26 XII Fulminata (Melitene)
27 XIII Gemina (Apulum)
28 XIV Gemina (Carnuntum)
29 XV Apollinaris (Satala)
30 XVI Flavia (Samosata)

31 XX Valeria Victrix (Deva)
32 XXII Primigenia (Mogontiacum)
33 XXX Ulpia (Castra Vetera)

Provinces

Italia
Provinces extant in the 1st century AD
Provinces created in the 2nd century AD

up the lands of the troublesome Chatti to the legions.

By AD 116, Trajan's campaigns had brought the Roman empire to its greatest extent (despite retrenchment in Britain), but only for a year. Hadrian's reorganization reverted almost to the Flavian frontiers, but the annexation of Dacia stood as a testament to Trajanic imperialism. After Domitian abandoned the conquest of Britain, only Antoninus Pius renewed the attempt, and ultimately failed. Augustus' frontiers on the Rhine and Danube remained largely intact, despite the reported intention of Marcus Aurelius to annex the territory of the Marcomanni and Quadi. In Africa, internal troubles and the external geography conspired

to restrict the Roman provinces to the coastal strip and its hinterland. It remained for Lucius Septimius Severus, in a new phase of empire, wholeheartedly to take the role of *propagator imperii* ('extender of the empire') that his predecessors had failed to adopt.

The army that Trajan inherited, however, was subtly different from Augustus', partly as a result of Claudius' reforms, and partly as a result of changing expectations. The legions had gradually forged their own identities and, by now, drew their manpower from

The Tropaeum Traiani ('Trajan's trophy') at Adamklissi, reconstructed in the 1970s, was dedicated to Mars 'the Avenger' in AD 108. It is thought to mark the site of a Domitianic disaster. A series of 54 individual panels (or 'metopes') depict scenes of Roman combat and victory over Dacian and Germanic warriors. (Dana T/ CC-BY-SA-3.0-RO)

provincials – the western legions largely from the Romanized inhabitants of Spain and Gaul, the eastern legions largely from those of Macedonia and Galatia – who had little or no idea of Rome and the senate. Their loyalty was to the emperor who paid them and looked after them. Only the Praetorians still, in the main, recruited Italians and maintained a bond with Rome. The new auxiliary units that proliferated in the frontier provinces identified even less with Rome; often recruited near their station, they equally often settled there after discharge, so that their idea of the Roman empire was restricted to their own patch of the frontier.

Throughout this period, the Roman empire was run by an administration that was chiefly civilian in character, despite the fact that the Roman nobility found their self-worth in the pursuit of *gloria* ('renown') and *virtus* ('excellence'). It is commonly remarked that the army that carved out the empire and defended its frontiers was commanded by amateurs. This is perhaps to misunderstand the difference between the tactical functioning of the Roman army, a force of well-drilled, well-equipped soldiers led by long-service centurions, and its strategic functioning, which was often the result of consultation between emperor and knowledgeable advisors. It also neglects the fact that none of Rome's adversaries fielded similarly professional armies.

Nevertheless, the genuine crises to afflict the empire came not from outside but rather from inside. The real dangers were posed,

not by Chatti or Dacians, nor by Jews or Parthians – although these might inflict heavy damage, the right man could always be found (eventually) to deal with these dangers, and new legions raised (eventually) to replace those destroyed. The real dangers were posed by the emperors themselves, and the lack of a sound process for selecting them. During the civil war of AD 69, the Roman world was fortunate that Vespasian ushered in a period of calm, sensible reorganization. Similarly, the excessive damage done by Trajan's eastern adventure was repaired by Hadrian, when it could easily have been exacerbated. But there was no guarantee that it would be thus. Fate took the sensible administration of Antoninus Pius and Marcus Aurelius, with their years of patient work, and handed it to Commodus for swift destruction.

Rarely did external factors play a critical part. The plague brought back from the east by Lucius Verus' army (which, but for the foolishness of a single senator, need not have been there at all) certainly wrought untold damage, when combined with wearisome years of battling on the northern frontier, at a time when the empire should have been enjoying the mature fruits of prosperity. On his deathbed, Marcus Aurelius, when asked for the final watchword by the sentry, advised him to 'go to the rising sun, for I am already setting' (Cassius Dio, *Roman History* 71.34.1). If he meant to indicate Commodus by this riddle, his advice was sadly misguided, as Commodus' day was indeed a dark end to this phase of the Roman Principate. It was left to another to forge a new kind of empire.

Further reading

The main ancient sources for the period of the Principate can be found in translation either in the Penguin Classics series or in the Loeb Classical Library.

The second edition of the *Cambridge Ancient History* provides the most reliable general background reading, and readers of this book are directed to volume 10 (*The Augustan Empire, 43 BC–AD 69*, edited by A.K. Bowman, E. Champlin & A. Lintott, Cambridge: Cambridge University Press, 1996) and volume 11 (*The High Empire, AD 70–192*, edited by A.K. Bowman, P. Garnsey & D. Rathbone, Cambridge: Cambridge University Press, 2000). Colin Wells' *The Roman Empire* (2nd edition, London: HarperCollins, 1992) is recommended as a concise and readable overview.

For the 'Portrait of a Soldier', the reader is referred to David Kennedy's article, 'C. Velius Rufus', in *Britannia* 14 (1983), pp. 183–96. For the 'Portrait of a Civilian', more detail can be found in *The Roman World of Dio Chrysostom*, by C.P. Jones (Cambridge, MA & London: Harvard University Press, 1978),

with the pertinent comments of K.R. Bradley in *The Classical Journal* 75 (1980), pp. 274–76. And for 'The World Around War', the reader will profit from Fergus Millar's article, 'The World of the *Golden Ass*', in *The Journal of Roman Studies* 71 (1981), pp. 63–75.

In this military narrative, I have attempted to take a prosopographical approach, tracing (in some small way) the actions of individuals from reign to reign, rather than simply concentrating upon the achievements of each reigning emperor. Many of these individuals are studied in greater depth in *The Roman Government of Britain*, by A.R. Birley (Oxford: Oxford University Press, 2005). More detail on the Roman army and its adversaries can be found in *The Roman Army at War 100 BC–AD 200*, by Adrian Goldsworthy (Oxford: Clarendon Press, 1996). Individual fortresses and forts, and the movements of the legions and auxiliary units, are covered in my previous Osprey books, *Roman Legionary Fortresses 27 BC–AD 378* (Oxford: Osprey, 2006) and *Roman Auxiliary Forts 27 BC–AD 378* (Oxford: Osprey, 2009).

Index

References to illustrations are shown in **bold**.